PRAISE FOR *FACI*

Facing Leviathan is a beautifully written book that weaves history and the Word of God together in a spectacular and challenging tapestry. I was moved, encouraged, and provoked.

MATT CHANDLER, *lead pastor of The Village Church in Dallas, Texas, president of Acts 29 Church Planting Network*

With a sharp historical analysis, Mark Sayers shows how we are shaped by a culture where image and performance is everything. This book is a must-read for brave leaders who want lead and live in a way that is shaped by the life of Jesus.

THOMAS WILLER, *sociologist, author, pastor of Regen, Copenhagen, Denmark*

Mark has written a beautifully engaging and well-researched book on culture that drips with the prophetic. His insights into cultural history and how we got here are breathtaking, and how he turns them into lessons on leadership is just brilliant. This book is fun, insightful, engaging . . . I could go on and on. If you are a leader in any capacity, read this book.

DAVE LOMAS, *pastor of Reality San Francisco, author of* The Truest Thing about You

Mark Sayers understands leadership far beyond the bite-sized axioms frequently used. By teaching with his own failures in leadership as a prime example, he has the experience necessary to show the danger of following the movement of the culturally mandated leadership. Take up the challenge of having your own preconceived notions of leadership questioned by reading *Facing Leviathan,* and walk away a leader who first follows the example of Christ, rather than the latest management tool.

TYLER BRAUN, *author of* Why Holiness Matters

Unlike any leadership book I have ever read, *Facing Leviathan* traverses the waves of Western history and exposes dangerous cultural currents in order to land us safely ashore a leadership that is neither pragmatic nor pietistic. Sayers charts a course right through the storms of vocational pride, ministry travails, and personal suffering by keeping a bead on God's profound, personal providence. Littered with insights, I couldn't shake the book after I read it. It haunted me, beckoning me into deeper self-reflection, while also inspiring me to lead underneath God. As you read, you'll get to think, repent, and refocus. On top of all that, it's a literary feast with morsels for all to enjoy.

JONATHAN K. DODSON, *lead pastor of City Life Church Austin, author of* Gospel-Centered Discipleship

If you're like me and thought that leadership was reserved for the elite, that you had to be a CEO to be an influencer, there's good news: You don't. And this book will show you how.

JEFF GOINS, *author of* The In-Between

The cultural and personal storms of our day are indeed raging, and few books will help us navigate them like *Facing Leviathan*. With prophetic insight and personal transparency, Mark Sayers steers leadership the way it should always go in a storm: the way of Christ Himself.

TIM CHADDICK, *pastor of Reality Los Angeles, author of* Better

No one will challenge your thinking more than Mark! I so appreciate both his insights and his passion to develop authentic disciples of Christ. We are in dire need of new ways to think about the development of disciples and leaders. They need to be the net results of a culture and community, as opposed to a new program or our quick-fix methods."

TERRY WALLING, *president, Leader Breakthru*

FACING
LEVIATHAN

**LEADERSHIP, INFLUENCE, AND
CREATING IN A CULTURAL STORM**

MARK SAYERS

MOODY PUBLISHERS

CHICAGO

All Scripture quotations are taken from the Holy Bible, New International Version®, NIV®. Copyright © 1973, 1978, 1984, 2011 by Biblica, Inc.™ Used by permission of Zondervan. All rights reserved worldwide. www.zondervan.com. The "NIV" and "New International Version" are trademarks registered in the United States Patent and Trademark Office by Biblica, Inc.™

Edited by Jesse Lipes
Interior design: Erik M. Peterson
Typesetting: Puckett Smartt
Cover design: Oak and Ink

Library of Congress Cataloging-in-Publication Data
Sayers, Mark.
  Facing Leviathan : leadership, influence, and creating in a cultural storm / Mark Sayers.
    pages cm
  Includes bibliographical references.
  ISBN 978-0-8024-1096-2
  1. Leadership—Religious aspects—Christianity. 2. Christian life. 3. Christianity and culture. I. Title.
  BV4597.53.L43.S29 2014
  253—dc23
                                            2013039481

All websites and phone numbers listed herein are accurate at the time of publication but may change in the future or cease to exist. The listing of website references and resources does not imply publisher endorsement of the site's entire contents. Groups and organizations are listed for informational purposes, and listing does not imply publisher endorsement of their activities.

We hope you enjoy this book from Moody Publishers. Our goal is to provide high-quality, thought-provoking books and products that connect truth to your real needs and challenges. For more information on other books and products written and produced from a biblical perspective, go to www.moodypublishers.com or write to:

Moody Publishers
820 N. LaSalle Boulevard
Chicago, IL 60610

3 5 7 9 10 8 6 4 2

Printed in the United States of America

CONTENTS

FOREWORD

I believe that the times we live in are some of the most challenging for leaders of the Christian church.

Challenging, because the culture we are called to minister in keeps moving at a breathtaking pace. Globalization, technology, travel, sexuality, family, the workplace, and faith have taken on a form that a generation ago would barely recognize. On top of that we live in an increasingly connected world, which only seems to complicate things. A nuclear Iran, a fragile European Union, an America in decline, and a militaristic China all make us struggle to help the church navigate her way through this sea of chaos. Trying to discern the ethics of Jesus, and live these faithfully feels like an overwhelming task. And with radical individualism and consumerism seeping into the very fabric of our lives, the narrow road seems all but covered with confusion and suspicion, while the broad road more accessible and attractive than ever.

Leaders have generally responded to these challenges in two ways.

The first response has been one of power through control. A purely pragmatic approach based on tangible outcomes and results. The leader is seen as an achieving hero who can take on the challenges of our time. They read secular experts, tap the latest proven psychological insights, implement the best practices from celebrity CEO's, cast vision, offer world class programs, and will and work their way through the spiritual desert. But after forty or so years of this sort of approach, many are left scratching their heads. Should the world be telling the church how to be the church? Do best practices in the business world translate well into the nuanced, spiritually animated, countercultural way of Jesus? Many are beginning to have their doubts. Much of this leadership has resulted in Christian pragmatism and celebrity, which has us looking to the exception as the norm, chasing trends instead of wisdom, and imitating people and contexts we have no chance of ever reproducing.

The second response has been one of skeptical critique. This sort of leader is seen as somewhat of an artistic genius who can deconstruct what's wrong from outside of the traditional church. His goal is to challenge through creativity and novelty, in a way that delights and surprises those locked in the evangelical framework. This leader can meld together culture, philosophy, art, and spirituality in a way that makes the church seem like a safe organic alternative to the harsh realities of our confusing world. The church becomes a kind of bohemian boutique with Jesus at the center, and His followers enjoying the benefits of spiritual growth and relational well-being. The personal journey, and individual story carry a new kind of authority, and our lives often become a text elevated above Scripture. But many who have led in this sort of environment are beginning to doubt too. Does this romantic view of community and faith actually make any real difference in the world? Are people learning to deny themselves, take up their cross, and follow Jesus in the midst of this? Has this become a new kind of cultural ghetto, where our tiny stories are not woven into a grand story of redemption, but a cynical side story of how much better we are than the traditional church?

And in the midst of these responses the Western Church has not fared well. She seems to perpetually limp behind the world in terms of its mission, theology, practice, and heart. Our prophetic voice into these larger cultural issues often feels like an echo and feedback loop of the popular culture we are called to speak into. Sure, there are experts with certainty on the way to reach our "post

Christian' world, yet time and time again, these voices speak to the stereotype rather than reality of the culture we live in. This has left many church leaders fatigued, discouraged, and paralyzed as to where to go from here.

Many believe there has to be another way to bear witness to and lead, the church of Jesus in our day. And I think this book presents a compelling way forward. Rather than simply critiquing and reacting to previous models of leadership, Mark Sayers makes a case for a kind of leadership rooted in the timeless wisdom and example of Christ. A leadership based on the way of the cross, which transcends both trend and technique. Mark stands as one who has personally experienced the shortfalls of both of the previous models of leadership, and has given his life, in an extremely secular context, to build a pathway forward.

In *Facing Leviathan*, Mark pulls the task of leadership out of the hands of the alpha male and the creative genius, and rightly restores it to the crucified hands of the risen Lord.

He points us back to the person, work, and way of Jesus above all else, and reminds us that it is ultimately Jesus who will build a church that will not be prevailed against in our time.

And that is good news, for weary and confused leaders, and a world that has lost its way.

JON TYSON

Jon Tyson is the lead pastor of Trinity Grace Church in New York City. Originally from Australia, Jon moved to the US twelve years ago. He works, lives, and serves in one of the largest cultural and future missionary contexts of the world, the urban center. Trinity Grace has five churches in New York City. He lives in Manhattan with his wife, Christy, and their two children. Twitter: @JonTyson

PART I

NEW LEADERSHIP IN A CHAOTIC CULTURE

Paris was vaguely aware that it had a terrible cellar under it . . . which teemed with . . . gargantuan sea monsters.

—VICTOR HUGO, *Les Miserables*

Myth is unmasked by the Word of God.

—HANS URS VON BALTHASAR, *The Scandal of the Incarnation*

THE CREATIVE LEADER

He sat silently as he looked out upon the French countryside, now bathed in darkness. It was almost one thirty in the morning. No one spoke. In the morning he would finally see Paris.

It was the culmination of a dream. The mecca for every artist. Somehow after all of this he still felt like an artist, despite the political responsibility now resting on his shoulders. He was no longer the outsider looking in, he was at the top. Yet, he knew that many of them still looked upon him with contempt in their eyes. Their looks, their intonations, their expressions made him aware that he did not fit. He knew they resented his leadership. He exposed their prejudices, brought to the surface everything that they despised. He was a foreigner, not born into privilege like them. He did not speak with their clipped, refined accent. They played by the book, followed tradition, and valued cool efficiency.

He stayed up late, hated paperwork, and was bad with details. He was emotive and unconventional. They went home to their neat houses in the suburbs with their perfect families. He, in contrast, lived a bohemian bachelor's life. While they were falling asleep next to their respectable wives in their respectable homes, he was up half the night, engrossed in music, watching films, and talking art.

That is why he kept them at a distance, surrounding himself with friends and workmates who were different. He preferred spending time with artists and visionaries rather than bureaucrats. He was more at home with animals, out in nature, with ordinary people, away from their backbiting. He was not interested in maintaining the status quo. Instead he dreamed of creating a new future for others. He understood that through harnessing the potential that new media brought, he could change things, allow people to live rich, communal, authentic lives connected to the land.

Still no one spoke. In the distance there was the dull music of a thunderstorm.

They arrived in Paris at five in the morning on an early flight. They had one day to see all that they could. He was flanked by two friends, one an architect and one a sculptor. They flew around Paris in a car, drinking in the feast of art and architecture. They traveled down the Champs-Élysées, on to the Trocadéro, and then to the Eiffel Tower. He became elated at the beauty of the opera house. Although he had never seen Garnier's masterpiece, he knew every square inch of the building by heart. He was in a creative's heaven. An artistic tour of Paris could not miss the bohemian neighborhood of Montmartre; here the creative leader and his friends visited the Basilique du Sacré Cœur. Atop the church high above Paris was a statue of St. Michael dressed as a knight, battling the biblical monster Leviathan—a metaphor for the battles that would come to define the creative leader's life, and the entire trajectory of Western culture.

Later that night when he was alone with his friend the architect, he said, "Wasn't Paris beautiful? . . . In the past I often considered whether we would not have to destroy Paris."[1] Adolf Hitler then went to bed.

HOW LEADERSHIP AND INFLUENCE CHANGED

This book is about leadership, influence, and creativity. When we talk about leadership in the West, Hitler's influence haunts us, palpably present though unmentioned. He is the model of leadership that we wish to avoid: a model of leadership rooted in power, abuse, violence, and coercion. The image of Hitler, standing on the podium in full military attire, spitting out venomous rhetoric, urging people on with a show of authoritarian force, changed at a fundamental level the way that we think and feel about the way leaders exert their influence. Public speaking was irrevocably altered. No longer would leaders simply tell people what to do. Any public figure making exclusive claims seemed to now be treading on dangerous ground. No longer would people look to those in authority as messianic figures with the ability to rescue society from the storms that face us. It was almost as if the poison that Hitler released into the world had infected our idea of leadership itself. The idea was seemingly tainted. It is therefore no surprise that we have turned to what appear to be new models of leadership.

WHY WE WANT TO BE ACTIVISTS, CREATIVES, AND INFLUENCERS, BUT NOT LEADERS

Today many of us want to influence, but not many of us wish to lead. We describe ourselves as activists, consultants, creatives, and entrepreneurs. We shy away from calling ourselves leaders, or even worse: managers. In the past, certain jobs carried a sense of prestige that flowed from their authority and responsibility; doctors, judges, clergy, bankers, and professors held tremendous weight in society. Their social influence was rooted in their perceived trustworthiness, their respectability. Virtually no one today desires respectability above all else. Such a term seems daunting. Ask yourself if you would rather that people described you as respectable or as cool, fun, and creative. Today, most people prefer hipness to prestige.

When we are given leadership positions, we try to dilute the hierarchical overtones of our roles with ironic job titles. The business magazine *Fast Company* has made popular such a practice by researching innovative companies and reporting actual leadership titles such as Head Monster, Master of Disaster, Crayon Evangelist, or Idea Ambassador. Pastors have not been immune to this trend. When asked about their roles, many downplay their jobs with all kinds of rhetorical wriggling. When we do have to lead, we attach a caveat to any hint of traditional leadership, which downplays our authority. We have "rockstar CEOs," "hipster pastors."

While we may have an aversion to leadership and organization, we still wish to influence, to effect change, and to create meaning. Technological advances like social networking have given us the impression that we can now have influence minus responsibility, leadership, and organization. Ori Brafman's book *The Starfish and the Spider* attempts to show how companies can be leaderless. Books such as Clay Shirky's *Here Comes Everybody*, Seth Godin's *Tribes*, and Don Tapscott and Anthony Williams's *Wikinomics* describe a world in which traditional modes of leadership and organization are superfluous, or at least are outmaneuvered by online mass movements. Shirky explains it as, "Never have so many people been so free to say and do so many things with so many other people."[2]

FROM LEADER TO INSPIRER

Journalist David Brooks, writing about this reimagined era of influence, notes that in this new environment, the leader "is no longer a chess grand master, an imposing, aloof figure moving pieces around the board. Now he or she is likely to be portrayed, and to portray himself or herself, as an inspirer, a motivator." Brooks argues contemporary influencers "want to show they are playful free spirits. . . . They are creators. They . . . experiment and dream."[3] The desire to avoid being seen as "normal" or "mainstream" is paramount. Our desire to be different flows down from leaders into their organizations, shaping corporate culture and especially reshaping how we arrange our buildings and workspaces into open planned offices that seemingly eschew the hierarchical implications of closed offices. A kind of bogeyman model of leadership operates in most people's minds, a set of Hitlerian cultural values to avoid.

OLD ("BAD") LEADERSHIP VS. NEW ("GOOD") LEADERSHIP

Today, if we do have to lead, there is an unspoken yet powerful set of attributes that we must conform to. To put it simply, there are a set of leadership attributes that are passé that we will call *the mechanical* and a grouping that are in fashion that we will name *the organic*. I choose the terms because they represent the widespread yet rarely articulated mood in our culture in which we prefer the natural, the warm, and the authentic rather than the cold, calculating, and the mathematical. So we watch commercials by technology giants filled with human faces, images of nature, and earthy folk music. Corporate coffee chains sell their coffee in a way that makes you feel like you just handpicked the beans yourself with the Ethiopian coffee farmer. The Christian philosopher Roman Guardini noted that this move reflected the desire in Western culture to find a new ethical way from the traditional Christian conception of biblical revelation to the natural, in which anything natural was automatically good.[4]

As we will discover, despite Guardini's warnings, so much of the contemporary Christian church has bought into this dualistic view of life and leadership.

Our culture has come so far toward the value of the new organic leadership listed on the right that they are unquestionably taken as correct. Countless books are written urging CEOs, leaders, and pastors to make the move personally and organizationally from the mechanical column to the organic column. Leaders must be more creative, more innovative, more relational, more spontaneous, more instinctive, more authentic. Organizations must become networked, more flexible, more fun, more fluid. The

MECHANICAL	ORGANIC
Power	Creativity
Mainstream	Radical
Dogmatic	Flexible
Task-Driven	Relational
Duty	Love
Dictatorial	Collaborative
Formal	Casual
Traditional	Revolutionary
Materialist	Spiritual
Directives	Conversation
Stability	Fluidity
Linear	Holistic
Conventional	Imaginative
Work	Play
Prestige	Cool
Organization	Communal
Success	Authenticity

fear is that if we do not make this shift, leaders and organizations will fade into an obscure death. Thus, to make these changes leaders must embrace their hordes of consultants and experts to secure this much-needed transition.

WHAT IF THE NEW IS NOT NEW?

These organic values represent the ideology of our day. They tell us something profound—not so much about how the world works but rather about how we *want* the world to work.

WE WANT TO MOVE AWAY FROM THE MORE RIGID MECHANICAL STYLE OF LEADERSHIP BECAUSE IT REPRESENTS THE RECENT PAST—MODERNITY—A STAGE WE HAVE "EVOLVED BEYOND."

We are told repeatedly that such values will not work in our time because they were shaped by a particular moment in history, the modern era. Yet the question that very few ask is: How have the highly prized organic values been shaped by *our* moment in history? What do they tell us about our unacknowledged prejudices and flaws? Is there a downside to our new mode of influencing, our trendy, "innovative" style of leading? As we will discover in this book, history tells us that there is.

HOW WE GOT IT WRONG

My entire life in ministry has been shaped by attempting to live out the values embodied in the right-hand, organic column. I can still clearly remember the moment when it all fell into place for me. It was the early to mid-nineties and I was young and fresh into ministry. I was attending a conference on mission in my hometown of Melbourne, Australia. The overwhelming theme that came through at the conference was that we were in "postmodern times"; out with the old modern era, in with the new postmodern era. Being the son of an architect, I had heard my dad use the word *postmodern* to describe buildings, but I had no idea what the term meant. The various speakers at the conference used the word to describe drastic shifts in our current culture. Gone were the modern period's values of reason, objective truth, homogeneity, and progress (the mechanical column), and rapidly replacing it was the postmodern period; one characterized by emotion, subjective truth, pluralism, and a suspicion of progress, structure, order, and control.

What was most shocking of all was the revelation that the church, particularly the contemporary evangelical church, had it wrong. The speakers shared their belief that the contemporary church was deeply shaped by the values of modernity—its systems, structures, and orientation. An orientation more informed by mechanical efficiency, models taken from the business world rather than from the Bible, and cultural cues shaped by marketing and mass culture. With the coming of the postmodern era, the contemporary evangelical church would find itself horribly irrelevant, conference speakers assured us. The solution was to first examine and deconstruct the ways in which contemporary Christianity had been co-opted by modernity. Second, to reach the new "postmodern generation" we must extricate ourselves out of the mechanical vices of the modern era and "incarnate" into postmodern culture; we must become postmodern Christians, postmodern churches, and postmodern leaders.

My head spun, not in shock but in delight. For someone who loved Jesus but felt culturally alien in the contemporary church, this was great news. For someone who at high school preferred alternative and indie music to mainstream music, who did well at art, drama, and literature but poorly at math, science, and well . . . generally that whole being organized thing, this was a ticket to freedom. For someone whose friends were miles from mainstream Christian culture, the rapidly oncoming influence of postmodernism was very welcomed. This was some kind of heavenly news. History was seemingly tilting in my favor. Freed from the mechanical vice, I could finally breathe.

This conference was just the tip of the iceberg. The trickle of Christian books announcing the coming of the postmodern epoch turned into a flood. I devoured most of them. At the time I was at a traditional church, so to reach this mysterious emerging group I decided to plant another congregation—a postmodern one. We ditched anything that seemed to reek of "contemporary church." Out went singing. In its place: experiential, multisensory worship. The traditional sermon went too, replaced by dialogue and clips from movies. We even changed the physical space in which we met, for a while creating an indoor faux-forest in which we sat around, elucidating upon the mysteries of Scripture, while ambient techno chirped along in the background. This was postmodernism in action. It was fluid, it was organic, and it was life-giving.

Soon what I was doing was discovered by older heads, who were proclaiming a new missionary approach to our postmodern culture. I became a supposed example of a genuine postmodern doing a new kind of ministry—a vision of the future. Still unformed and largely untested as a leader, yet with a whiff of the new circulating around me, I began to receive speaking engagements and invitations to speak into the future of churches and organizations. I was sought out to interpret the landscape of this bold, new, postmodern terrain.

Through the postmodern movement, an alternate Christian universe was growing up alongside mainstream church culture. Where the latter was steeped in theological structures and dogma, the former was defined culturally. It took very seriously the culture we inhabit and to which we are called to witness—the postmoderns. For the church to have any relevance in this new era, it was vital that it relinquished older patterns and structures and embraced the postmodern. Thus the word *postmodernism* seemed to take on a power of its own in the Christian world, operating something like the Jedi mind trick, used to justify any kind of reformist agenda.

The organic values stem from this postmodern era. Dogma gave way to flexible exploration, hierarchy was replaced by a network of laterally defined relationships, authority and authoritative claims were viewed with suspicion. Eventually, we believed that mainstream culture would disappear altogether, replaced by the way more appealing, easier-going organic principles.

Still green and in my early twenties, I traveled to the United States to speak about this brave new postmodern world to an American evangelical organization. Soon America would join this conversation, where it would expand and amplify, spawning whole movements and vast libraries of books. For the next fifteen or so years, I lived out the conviction that the postmodern world had changed everything. Through my leadership I would attempt to embody the organic values in a variety of missional movements and innovative plants. Yet, something was amiss. The organic values were not delivering the idealized world that they had seemingly promised.

I had delivered speeches. I had started ministries. I had embodied the fluid, the creative. I could criticize the status quo like a champion. I was a poster boy for a new kind of young, emerging leader. Except that after a decade of launching, birthing, and pioneering, there was little left standing.

SWAMPED BY CHAOS

I was confronted by the surprising fruitlessness I felt after I took a position as the senior leader of a missional church renowned for its creativity and innovation. I had been with the church for some time, yet now leading the church I began to wonder if we would survive. We embodied all the highly esteemed organic values, yet chaos seemed to be overtaking us. Despite the alarm bells I ignored this reality, insisting that the organic values would eventually become a catalyst for growth and change within the church.

One day not long after the birth of my first child, my wife, Trudi, turned to me and asked if our church was going to be around when our daughter was fourteen. I was silenced by this question as I was forced to confront the answer: a resounding no. Although strong on the fluid, the relational, and the creative, we did not have the organizational strength or resilience to continue. We were recognized for our revolutionary spirit, our imagination, hipness, and creativity, but we didn't have the structures and the leadership to sustain, cultivate, and grow it over the long haul.

By this stage the postmodern movement had been progressing for over a decade. However, the average community centered upon its philosophy only lasted an average of three years. Our church was one of the few still remaining and I could not stand the thought of pouring so much pastoral and ministry energy into it only to have it slowly fade away. In essence we knew what we did not want to be—a modern, mainstream contemporary church—but conversely, we also did not know what we wanted to be. This was all new terrain and it was starting to show serious cracks. Just as disturbingly, when I looked around this new Christian cadre of which I was a part, it may have been filled with highly esteemed, creative, innovative thinkers, but it also was filled with broken lives. Instead of growing disciples, we were giving people permission to grow lax in their faith. We had heroically rallied together to reach what we saw as the chaotic postmodern culture, yet ironically instead of us reaching it, its chaos had seemingly swamped us. I was left dazed, disorientated, and confused.

I started to experience a faith crisis—not my faith in Christ but my faith in the organic values I had become well known for. I began to ask questions in the context of our postmodern Christian culture and realized that if my church was going to survive—if I was going to survive—I could no longer blindly lead from the postmodern, organic values.

It was then that I was reminded of a deeply disturbing comment made at that very first conference on postmodernism in Melbourne over ten years prior. It had stuck dormant within me and now could not be ignored. It was made by one of the speakers, an older and respected pastor. He said that he felt that the shift toward the postmodern in our culture had created a climate in which a dictator could influence the current generation. I had been enjoying his presentation till that point. I vehemently disagreed with him. The postmodern, organic values that we were moving toward seemed a natural insulation against such a rise to power. Yet all these years later I would discover that there was truth in the speaker's point. Our culture shaped by the organic values was now ripe for exploitation. Just as there were dangers in the mechanical values of the left-hand column, the organic values of the right hand also contained seeds of destruction.

THE ENLIGHTENMENT AND THE CULTURAL SPLIT

The mechanical and organic columns reveal a split in our culture between competing worldviews. These two visions of reality offer us two types of leadership and influence. They are both broad and hard to pin down. To understand them we must paint in broad brushstrokes. One camp sprang from the period of Western history known as the Enlightenment, which spanned the seventeenth and eighteenth centuries, while the other surfaced as a reaction to the first. This period broke with the West's traditional past, which was built upon a fusion of Greek thinking and Christianity. As the term illustrates, the proponents of the Enlightenment saw themselves as bringing light to a culture living in the darkness of violence and superstition. The Enlightenment was not sparked by one moment. Rather it was a catalogue of discoveries and paradigm shifts that reconstituted the West's entire understanding of reality.

THE ENLIGHTENMENT RECAST THE DRAMA OF HUMAN EXISTENCE WITH THE INDIVIDUAL PLAYING THE LEAD ROLE.

This drama was guided by a newfound optimism, which was itself rooted in the rationality of the human mind. Reason would now lead society beyond superstition and that which cannot be empirically proven. New scientific discoveries aided by rapidly developing technologies would create a kind of human-driven heaven on earth. God was not immediately removed from the picture. However, a profound shift had occurred: no longer was faith directed primarily toward God. Instead, Western society faith shifted toward the power and potential of humankind. Such a worldview increasingly marginalized the Christian faith. The Enlightenment would eventually create the possibility for people in the West to live without a belief in God or the supernatural. A machine became the most appropriate metaphor to apply to humanity, the movements of the universe, and society itself. The Enlightenment directly shaped the values of the mechanical column. Thus, in the imagination of the Enlightenment with its mechanical values, the leader par excellence is a successful hero figure: powerful, commanding, and conquering, creating with determination, organization, and systems as powerful as the hero himself.

THE REACTION

These monumental cultural changes reshaped the West at every level. There was a desire to make a clean break with the past; inherited tradition was questioned, social structures critiqued. The modern world was being born. Naturally, those wedded to the traditional worldview of the West found this ground shift traumatizing. Some wished to return to the past, yet another group wanted a different vision of the future to emerge. This group began to find faults with the trajectory of the Enlightenment, questioning whether human reason was the only way of comprehending the world. This group wondered if the mechanical approach to life was re-creating man as a kind of robot, devoid of emotions, a sense of beauty, and meaning. They feared that the skepticism of the Enlightenment worldview robbed humans of the spiritual, the sensual, and the cultivation of the soul. They started a countermovement known as Romanticism.

In part, Romanticism arose in reaction to the Enlightenment. Yet it did not advocate returning to a Christian worldview based on Scripture and revelation. Romanticism attempted to create an alternative to the mechanical worldview. It would base its ideology on the suspicion of power and structure, a view that would pronounce the natural over the technical. They preferred emotion and experience

to reason and the empirical. They held spirituality above material-
ism. Essentially the organic values are shaped by Romanticism. The
romantic vision, with its organic values, imaged the leader and the
influencer to not be the achieving hero of the Enlightenment but
rather the creative genius who influences through innovation, art,
and dangerously brilliant ideas. The Romantic vision imagines the
creative genius as a heretic, always pushing boundaries and breaking taboos. Thus, in the organic vision, the creative creates but they
also tear down. As we will discover, this is a very different view from
the biblical idea of creativity.

For the sake of clarity, for the remainder of this book I will refer
to Enlightenment values as the mechanical, and the values of Romanticism as the organic. These two visions have been at battle in
our culture now for centuries. The organic values do not originate
in the 1960s but rather in the eighteenth century. They are still at
war in our culture today and they are responsible for much of the
storm of chaos that has beset our culture. They plaster over our
culture a binary view of the world—counterculture vs. mainstream,
hipster inner city vs. white suburbs, liberal vs. conservative, indie
vs. pop, arthouse vs. Hollywood, mall vs. boutique, fast food vs.
organic, Microsoft vs. Apple, the Coast vs. the Midwest.

I and so many others misread the culture when we believed that
the organic values were the outbreak of a new era, that they represented a new postmodern epoch in the West. Yes, postmodernism was and is an academic movement, but it was never an epoch.
When Christians bought this analysis, it deeply affected the way we
viewed leadership. Many who rightfully questioned the way that the
mechanical values had shaped the contemporary Christian view of
leadership saw an alternative in the organic values, and they jumped
across. Such a move seemed to have all the airs of a conversion experience. Thus, the language of the binary battle between the mechanical and the organic values began to invade the contemporary

Christian discussion. What on the surface seemed to be theological or missiological discussions, such as the debate between proponents of contemporary churches and emerging churches, or missional and mega churches, were in fact deeply shaped by the cultural battle between the mechanical and organic values.

This ensured that our current view of Christian leadership was also shaped by this battle between the mechanical values' model of the successful hero who builds and organizes, and the organic values' vision of the creative genius who ideates and critiques. It is my deep conviction, as this book will attest, that both the heroic and the genius models of leadership are flawed. Both are compromised and corrupted by the worldview from which they emerged: paganism. I am not speaking of the modern Wiccan movement but the dominant worldview of the Greek and Roman worlds. A worldview that the minority Christian movement found itself surrounded by. A worldview that still deeply influences our culture today. We often miss this precisely because that is part of the nature of paganism.

Historian Robin Lane Fox notes that while the Christian faith was centered on a definite sense of faith and commitment to the belief that God has revealed Himself in history in the person of Jesus Christ, in contrast, pagan belief was assumed. It held no doctrine, no creeds, and it was opposed to a breaking in of God in history. Instead, it simply existed in the air; it was part of the fabric of society that silently shaped how culture acted and behaved.[5] Thus, its influence is still with us today.

The revolt against Christianity that came with the advent of the modern world was, in the words of historian Peter Gay, the rise of modern paganism—a reaching back into the world that predated Christianity. Built upon polytheism and resting upon a myriad of different gods, paganism was a divided house. It could contain both Apollos, a heroic god of power and order, and Dionysius, a creatively chaotic bohemian god of pleasure.[6] Thus, both the hero and the genius can be found in pagan conceptions of what it is to influence and lead.

The real battle in which our culture is engaged is not between the mechanical and the organic but rather between the pagan and Christian worldviews. A Christianity that attempts to model itself on the hero or the genius will be a faith that has little potential to speak good news to the West. Instead, we must rediscover the truly radical vision of leadership found within the Bible. A model of leadership born out of a dangerous truth that was repellant to pagan ears. A truth that dared to proclaim in pagan streets and squares that God had lowered Himself to come and live in the mess and muck of human life, within history, in time, in human flesh. The pagans wished to leave this world, to cross the divide between human and god. Whether it be through power or pleasure, they wanted to get out. But the dangerous gospel taught that the central organizing principle for leadership, for life, for the universe, was the truth that God had come to us. That He had died upon a cross, spilling His blood in love, paying a price before rising from the grave and ascending to heaven. All leadership must pass through this narrow gate. This truth jarred with the pagan world still jars in our modern pagan world.

The pagans could not stand the idea that God acted within history. They preferred neat ideas that hung in the ether. However, to return to a biblical understanding of leadership, creating, and influence, and to understand what it is to lead in the culture of the West, we must delve back into history . . . and literature. Specifically, France in the nineteenth century.

PART II

THE MONSTER IN THE DEEP

Imitate Paris, you will ruin yourself.

—VICTOR HUGO, *Les Miserables*

THE SEA MONSTER AND THE STORM

"The year 1866 was signalized by a remarkable incident, a mysterious and inexplicable phenomenon, which doubtless no one has yet forgotten."[1] So begins French novelist Jules Verne's *20,000 Leagues Under the Sea*, released upon a Paris public in 1870. The remarkable incident imagined in Verne's novel was the mysterious appearance of a sea monster that had attacked an ocean liner. The monster moves at an incredible rate of knots and is far larger than any known whale.

In the novel, the world's attention is gripped by the reports. "In every place of great resort the monster was the fashion. They sang of it in the cafes, ridiculed it in the papers, and represented it on the stage. All kinds of stories were circulated regarding it."[2] The monster's appearance enflames existing cultural battles within French society—battles over issues of science, religion, progress, the place of tradition, the direction of the country. The cultural storm that was unleashed by the French Revolution of 1789, which had roared out of France and across Europe and North Africa, still howled at the French capital. This new state, which had thrown off millennia of tradition and history, was at war with itself, still wrestling with the consequences of its own creation. The English philosopher Thomas Hobbes had used the biblical motif of the great and fearsome sea monster Leviathan to describe the state. Verne uses the motif of the biblical sea monster as a driving symbol in his story.

SUBMARINE AS A MODEL OF CULTURE

"There appeared in the papers caricatures of every gigantic and imaginary creative, from the white whale, the terrible 'Moby Dick' of hyperborean regions, to the immense kraken whose tentacles could entangle a ship of five hundred tons, and hurry it into the abyss of the ocean."[3] Verne references both Herman Melville's novel *Moby Dick*, published nineteen years earlier, and older tales of sea monsters that reach back to the ancient world. In the Old Testament, as in the literature of Israel's surrounding neighbors, sea monsters represented the primal chaos in the world that threatened at any time to burst forth and overwhelm creation. As the reader soon discovers, Verne's sea monster is not a creature, but rather a mechanical beast, a submarine named *Nautilus*. The submarine is a self-contained world filled with luxuries and comfort. Verne uses the *Nautilus*, the mechanical beast, as a metaphor of modern culture itself, brilliantly capturing its complexities and paradoxes, promises and threats. The submarine represents humankind's triumph over nature; it celebrates our ability to travel anywhere, even to the deep and dark places we once feared, all the while sealed in furnished comfort. The submarine represents the modern West's attempts, through its own guile and effort, to shape a life protected from the storms that lash at humankind.

THE LEADER WHO TURNS HIS BACK ON THE WORLD

The *Nautilus* is captained by Nemo, an Indian prince who has given up his title and identity for a new life of influence and leadership. Turning his back on both politics and dry land, Nemo has reinvented himself as a man of science, exploring the oceans. When questioned about his relationship to society, Nemo replies, "I am not what you call a civilised man! I have done with society entirely, for reasons that I alone have the right of appreciating. I do not therefore obey its laws."[4] For a man who has spurned civilization, he is paradoxically a connoisseur of the fruits of Western society. The *Nautilus* contains a vast library of the world's classics, an art gallery complete with works by Renaissance masters and French neo-classicists. The submarine even contains a large organ upon which the captain plays Wagner and Beethoven. He wishes to spurn culture, locking himself in a submarine instead of contributing, but also wants to enjoy its treasures. Nemo's intentions are conflicted. His scientific voyages are funded by his looting of shipwrecks, yet he sometimes uses his stolen gains to support those fighting for their freedom against imperial nations. Nemo seems to be driven by the idea of raw freedom:

"The sea does not belong to despots. Upon its surface men can still exercise unjust laws, fight, tear one another to pieces . . . But at thirty feet below its level, their reign ceases, their influence is quenched and their power disappears. Ah! Sir, live—live in the bosom of the waters! There only is independence! There I recognise no masters! There I am free!"[5]

Yet ironically, because of the nature of submarines, Nemo is imprisoned in his vessel. Forever on the run, he frees the oppressed yet keeps prisoners in his ship. His ship, a wonder of technology and scientific power, takes him across the world to the depths of the ocean. Yet he remains in exile from humanity and even relationally from his crew. In Nemo, Verne asked a powerful question of how power and leadership were to be framed and exercised in the emerging modern world, a world that was shedding tradition, convention, and authority. Verne wrote of his character, "Not only had he put himself beyond the pale of human laws, but he had made himself independent of them, free in the strictest acceptation of the word, quite beyond their reach! . . . No man could demand from him an account of his actions; God, if he believed in one—his conscience, if he had one—were the sole judges to whom he was answerable."[6]

As the modern age jettisoned traditions, it also turned its back on commonly held senses of morality and justice. Behind the technological prowess and potential of the *Nautilus*, it still bears the shape of those ancient sea monsters, symbolic of chaos.

The *Nautilus* emerges as a model of a self-contained society, reflecting the new Paris. This new Post-Revolutionary Paris attempted to create a self-contained world, to be a comfortable shelter from the cultural storm. It would also create a new kind of citizen, the modern—one who wished to pursue her own agenda, to live a life of freedom and pleasure away from the chaos. Yet as Nemo's crew discovered, their protective ship was a sea monster itself. It had the potential to protect, but its hull was shaped like the sea monster of chaos, captained by a conflicted yet heroic leader, roaming the open sea.

THE SEA

The *Nautilus* is protected from the physical dangers of the sea by a storm glass. However, in the biblical imagination, as in many other forms of literature, the sea represents chaos, death, and the unknown—a place of separation from life and God. As his ship cuts through the icy depths, Verne's Captain Nemo finds himself squarely within this narrative of disorder and disconnection. In the book of Job, the sea is portrayed as a body of chaos God needs to reign in.

Who shut up the sea behind doors
  when it burst forth from the womb,
when I made the clouds its garment
  and wrapped it in thick darkness,
when I fixed limits for it
  and set its doors and bars in place,
when I said, "This far you may come and no farther;
  here is where your proud waves halt"? (Job 38:8–11)

The expansive oceans are described as "proud." The powerful sea does and goes wherever it pleases until God provides limitations. In Genesis, as the chaos of sin overtakes the world, the flood occurs when God removes His hand that holds back the waters. When the bars and doors that God has placed over the sea are removed, the chaos is let loose.

On that day all the springs of the great deep burst forth, and the floodgates of the heavens were opened. And rain fell on the earth forty days and forty nights. . . . The waters rose and increased greatly on the earth, and the ark floated on the surface of the water. They rose greatly on the earth, and all the high mountains under the entire heavens were covered. The waters rose and covered the mountains to a depth of more than fifteen cubits. Every living thing that moved on land perished—birds, livestock, wild animals, all the creatures that swarm over the earth, and all mankind. (Genesis 7:11–12, 18–21)

Due to the destructive force of sin, the earth is consumed by the power of the sea. The world seemingly returns to the watery, formless chaos it was at creation. God does not only create: He holds back destruction. In Scripture we see images of God triumphing over the sea, as in Moses leading the people out of Egypt and splitting the waters, Jonah's grand escape being intercepted by a storm, or Jesus commanding the raging sea to be quiet. From a biblical perspective, by attempting to enjoy cultural pleasures while simultaneously removing itself from all social and political entanglements, Nemo's *Nautilus* represents an attempt to hold back the sea, not by the power of God but by the hand of man. The *Nautilus* dwells in the middle of pure formlessness, attempting to subsist on nothing more than its own provisions and sheer determination. Nemo—ensconced safely in his mechanical wonder, leading with authority, given godlike power by technology—at times heroically intervening in history, at other times holding the world at a stoic distance. This captain is the model of mechanical leadership.

THE OTHER BOAT

Another Frenchman, the twentieth-century literary critic Roland Barthes, noted that Verne's novel and especially the metaphor of the *Nautilus* conveyed a vision of life in which man was in complete control of the world:

> Verne in no way sought to enlarge the world by romantic ways of escape or mystical plans to reach the infinite: he constantly sought to shrink it, to populate it, to reduce it to a known and enclosed space, where man could subsequently live in comfort: the world can draw everything from itself . . . for it is enough to present the ship as the habitat of man, for man to immediately to organize there the enjoyment of a round, smooth universe, of which, in addition, makes him at once the god, the master, and the owner.[7]

For Barthes, Verne's vision of Captain Nemo, turning his back on the world's cultures and attempting to create a new society in his controlled, self-sufficient submarine epitomized modernity's worldview. The idea of captain Nemo, comfortably ensconced in the drawing room of the *Nautilus*, pipe and book in hand, was the embodiment of a kind of modern, middle-class myth. Nemo, hidden beneath the world, cherishing his dream of complete liberty, free from relational entanglement and the messiness of the real world was for Barthes the vision of a man-child. A man who had created a boy-like cubbyhole where no one will tell him what to do "while outside the storm . . . rages."[8]

At the end of his essay that harshly critiques Verne's worldview as expressed in Nemo and the *Nautilus*, Barthes professed that he preferred a different metaphor for life and influence. It was a poem by Arthur Rimbaud titled "The Drunken Boat." The poem, like Verne's work, also uses the metaphor of a seafaring craft. However, this vessel is not the embodiment of a modern, middle-class myth of comfort and control. Rather "The Drunken Boat" describes the aimless drifting of an abandoned boat. This ghost ship narrates its own journey. With no purpose, direction, crew, or captain it can only catalogue what it experiences and sees. Like *20,000 Leagues Under the Sea*, "The Drunken Boat" also references the ancient biblical images of storms and the sea monster Leviathan. Yet instead of hiding from the storm in comfort, like Nemo, the ship recounts that "The storm made bliss of my sea-borne awakenings. Lighter than a cork, I danced on the waves."[9]

The ship's purposeless, leaderless wandering reduced its existence to a meaningless series of experiences and sights to behold. The ship is battered by the waves, eventually sinking into the emptiness of the deep. At the end of the poem there is a lament for youth before the ship finally meets its doom. The ship does not learn, it does not mature, it only experiences.

Rimbaud wrote "The Drunken Boat" in 1871 after reading *20,000 Leagues Under the Sea*. Rimbaud was just sixteen when he composed the work, which to this day is still considered groundbreaking. Rimbaud was a teen star of an artist circle known as The Decadents, a group who despised the morality of the emerging middle class. The Decadents were part of a larger social group who mocked technological progress, who looked not for comfort from the storm, but rather to be tossed and thrown by its turbulence. In contrast to the heroism of Nemo, they offered another form of cultural influence, one born of breaking cultural taboos. A mode of leadership driven by heresy, theirs was a cult of creativity. True inheritors of the legacy of the French Revolution, they wanted to upturn the world, tear apart its conventions and traditions.

Rimbaud traveled from his childhood home to Paris in his late teens, entering into both the city's creative underbelly and a tempestuous homosexual relationship with the older poet Paul Verlaine. Staying true to his life philosophy as expressed in "The Drunken Boat," Rimbaud drifted around the world in an experiential haze, addicted to drugs and alcohol. The brilliant poet would also be known for his terrible, childish behavior, including one drunken fight with Verlaine in which his older lover shot the teenage Rimbaud in the arm. Jules Verne, in comparison to Rimbaud, led a life of social propriety. However, like the decadent poet, he would also be shot. Unlike his creation Nemo, who was able to hide from the chaotic storms of real life, Verne was shot in the leg by his psychologically disturbed nephew.

The two writers offered two competing versions of how life should be led and how one should influence the modern culture. Verne's response was founded in reason, of the mastery of both nature and emerging technology. In the character of Nemo, Verne attempted to transport a mechanical model of leadership and character into the contemporary world. On the other hand, Rimbaud's model of a captain-less boat, drifting atop the world's chaotic currents and attempting to hold on to youth, set adrift from tradition and direction, also marked a new approach to life. It was an attempt to influence.

These two contradictory characters shared two other things in common besides being shot. First, both men abandoned their once-pious Christian faith. Rimbaud would seemingly abandon God altogether, giving himself over to hedonism. Verne would abandon belief in Christ, preferring to believe in a distant god whose loose and mysterious influence in the world would be through the providential action of great heroes like Nemo. Verne would attempt to defeat Leviathan by controlling it, by turning it into a mechanical agent of providence in the world. Rimbaud would prefer to give himself over as a sacrifice to the chaotic sea monster, to be subsumed into the deep. Religion aside, the second commonality the two writers had was, like so many others of their craft, they would both be drawn to the cultural magnetism of Paris.

PART III

PARIS: THE FIRST SOCIETY OF THE SPECTACLE

Paris, this model city, this blueprint of the well-made capital that every nation tries to copy, this metropolis of the idea . . . this centre and home of the mind, this nation city, this hive of the future.

—VICTOR HUGO, *Les Miserables*

Can you pull in Leviathan with a fishhook or tie down its tongue with a rope? . . . If you lay a hand on it, you will remember the struggle and never do it again! Any hope of subduing it is false; the mere sight of it is overpowering.

—JOB 41:1, 8–9

THE CULTURAL STORM

Paris at the end of the nineteenth century was the epicenter of the cultural storm of modernity, a maelstrom of competing visions and influences of how society should frame what the modern world should be. This period of comparative peace and prosperity and cultural flowering would be known as the *Belle Epoque*, in English, "the beautiful era." It would also be known by another term, which carried an apocalyptic and morally degenerate tinge, the *fin de siècle*, or the "end of the century."

Paris was a city in which two competing forms of modern culture were at war in a monstrous battle for the future. The mechanical vision was founded in heroic action that would progress toward a utopian future of freedom, aided by pragmatism, reason, technology, and power. The other vision, the organic, was a reaction to the mechanical, a rebellion of the emotive, the sensate, the irrational, and the primitive. This organic vision did not so much seek a utopian liberty, insomuch as a communal gathering of liberated individuals, pursuing pleasure, creating art, defying convention, and inhabiting on the cultural margins.

As we will discover as we journey together through this book, these two visions are still at battle in our day, shaping our contemporary world. We will also discover that while this battle is at the heart of our contemporary culture, it is also an ancient battle. It is the reinvocation of two great ancient heresies, one rooted in an attempt to reach for heroic godlikeness, the other a bowing before the sea monster of the chaotic deep.

THE IMPORTANCE OF PARIS

The mechanical and the organic do not exist in neatly separated boxes; they intertwine and play off of each other. The real story however does not recount one age beginning and another ending, but Western culture consisting of both the mechanical and the organic, creating a cultural storm. This cultural storm affected all of the modern West, but it was Paris that became the chief staging ground for the development of the organic and the mechanical values. The great cultural critic Walter Benjamin believed that understanding Paris in the second half of the nineteenth century was the key to understanding the cultural storm that had beset Western culture, as demonstrated in his literary project *Arcades Project*. Benjamin saw the city as a kind of text to be read and interpreted. He found himself unwillingly in Paris. As a German Jew, he had been forced to leave his country with the rise of the Nazi regime. So important was his reading of the City of Light that as the jackbooted Nazi troops marched toward the French capital, Benjamin frantically wrote, recording his cultural interpretations, his typewriter pouring out words describing how Paris in the nineteenth century transformed from a traditional city into a kind of dream world built not upon reality but upon fantasy; a new kind of society centered not upon family, religion, and convention, but instead sex, shopping, and entertainment. Benjamin prophetically noted that this new kind of city promised individual freedom and sensation— it offered spectacle. The French thinker Guy Debord, writing in 1960's Paris, would describe modern culture as a "society of the spectacle"—people became passive observers, lured by its ostentatious flow, only to end up bored and alienated.

The specter of the approaching German army hovers over Benjamin's work, his words acting like defensive weapons, exposing the roots of the "society of the spectacle" that had been invaded by the grotesque theatre that was Nazism. Benjamin would never finish his work; his choice to take his life rather than face deportation to a concentration camp casts a tragic and prophetic pallor over his cultural analysis. So, following in Benjamin's footsteps as we attempt to understand what it is to lead and create in our own culture, we must travel back in time to the city that surprised and inspired Benjamin. We must return to Paris, exploring different historical moments, interacting with some of its prominent thinkers, and analyzing various themes as they relate to the development of modern culture and its effect on leadership.

A FESTIVAL OF EMANCIPATION

There were many strange and exotic sights in Paris in 1889, but this was one of the more unusual. A group of American Indians, many who had traveled straight from the interior of the United States, were offered a tour of the sights of Paris. The group was part of Buffalo Bill's Wild West show, which was one of the major draw cards at the Exposition Universelle, or World Exposition.

The Exposition was a world fair, a chance for countries to show off the fruits of their culture, their industry, their technological advances. The Expositions were giant, three-dimensional teaching spaces, propaganda machines that simultaneously sang the praise of empire, technology, the arts, consumerism, fashion, and entertainment. World fairs were almost like a nineteenth-century version of the Internet, reducing the world's culture, knowledge, and entertainment into one place. One could view exotic plants from a faraway jungle, marvel at the novelty of hearing a recorded voice on a phonograph, view a daringly modern impressionist painting, be captivated by Balinese dancers, enjoy a cup of Moroccan tea in a faux North African building, all before the pinnacle experience of climbing the Eiffel Tower to gaze across Paris. For a nineteenth-century person, it was a dizzying experience.

The primary purpose of these World Expositions according to Benjamin was to amuse in a "festival of emancipation." For Paris in the second half of the nineteenth century, the Exposition became an addiction for its fragile government, its citizens, and the millions of tourists who would pour through the gates. Expositions were held seventeen times throughout the second half of the nineteenth century. They were hugely popular, illustrating the optimistic belief in the potential of progress and technology at the time. They marked the first era of globalization, as countries from across the world, driven by nationalistic pride, showcased their culture and development. The Expositions acted as the heralds of the modern age. Their frequency did nothing to dampen the public's appetite, it only seemed to increase their enthusiasm. As Benjamin states in *Arcades Project*, "World exhibitions glorify the exchange value of the commodity. They create a framework in which its use value recedes into the background. They open a phantasmagoria which a person enters in order to be distracted. The entertainment industry makes this easier by elevating this person to the level of the commodity. He surrenders to its manipulations while enjoying his alienation from himself and others."[1]

THE EIFFEL TOWER

The Native Americans were given the grand tour, boarding a tram that took them past the sights of the grand boulevards, the Champs Elysées, the Bastille, and the Louvre. The group was taken through the Exposition itself, through the technological wonders of the Gallery of Machines, which featured such innovative technologies as sound recording and movie projection. The Native Americans, like almost any other visitor to the Exposition of 1889, were dumbstruck by the giant, iron tower erected in Paris that year. It was the tallest structure on earth, dwarfing the cathedrals that had previously held the record—in size and ideology. The Eiffel Tower was designed to be the entranceway into the exhibition, a stunning example of the power of science and technology.

For the citizens of Paris, the most dominating feature of the Exposition of 1889 was the iron tower created by Gustav Eiffel. To imagine Paris without the tower is impossible now. It was both literally and culturally a lightning rod. To the traditionalists, the tower was an aesthetic and spiritual abomination, a Leviathan setting its face and the people against God. Not only did it loom over Paris like a naked iron skeleton, casting its shadow across the city's churches and cathedrals, it was an alternate symbol to the cross, erected to celebrate the French Revolution. Many worried that it was a modern day version of Babel.

Technology and science had now, in the minds of many replaced the need for God. For the American writer Henry Adams, his visit to the Gallery of Machines was a religious experience. Describing this moment using third person in his autobiography, *The Education of Henry Adams*, he wrote of the "dynamo," a term he made popular representing the overwhelming awe of technological advance, as a rival to the Christian cross. "He began to feel the forty-foot dynamos as a moral force, much as the early Christians felt the Cross. The planet itself seemed less impressive, in its old-fashioned, deliberate, annual or daily revolution, than this huge wheel, revolving within arm's length. . . Before the end, one began to pray to it; inherited instinct taught the natural expression of man before silent and infinite force."[2]

The mechanical worldview was in the ascendancy.

FROM LEADERSHIP TO CELEBRITY

Paris was a political city. It was the birthplace of the French Revolution, the move away from the rule of monarchs and toward the rule of the people. It was a city of revolutionary action, in which citizens would regularly take to the streets to demand political change. However the Expositions marked a dramatic shift, a groundbreaking change in how leadership and influence would be understood in the modern world. This shift moved from older understandings of leadership rooted in politics and the rule of law, toward the idea of celebrity as the primary form of influence.

At the beginning of 1889—the year of the Exposition—it appeared the French government may fall. General Boulanger was a popular politician and general who had attempted to seize control of the government. Boulanger was the epitome of the old world style of leadership. For a while it looked as if Boulanger's revolution would succeed as he rode upon a wave of popular support. However by the midway point of the year, Boulanger had fled France. The Eiffel Tower and the Exposition had created an atmosphere of excitement, seemingly eclipsing the revolutionary spirit. Caught up in the buzz and thrill, the public had forgotten about the populist General Boulanger and instead were now enamored by Buffalo Bill, who made his name fighting in the American Indian Wars. He now toured the world with his "Wild West" show, in which he reenacted his battles. What was most bizarre about his performances was that Buffalo Bill would re-create his former battles with the actual Indians that he had fought against in real life. It was a strange development, one that would come to mark the modern age of spectacle: men who at one time were attempting to maim and kill each other were now performing a pantomime of their former deadly actions.

General Boulanger embodied leadership based upon honor, action, and positional power. Buffalo Bill represented a new kind of influencer, a celebrity, whose persona was rooted in imagery, performance, and illusion. The Republic that the French Revolution created asked citizens to serve their country. Now a new kind of understanding was emerging in Paris, in which society existed to serve and entertain the individual. Citizens were morphing into consumers.

GENTRIFICATION

Paris in 1889 did not simply host an Exposition, it *became* an exposition, a new kind of city to which people flocked, not to find a home but to be entertained, a place to reinvent themselves. Urban planner Georges-Eugène Haussmann helped facilitate this change by turning this once impoverished city into the Paris we know today. Haussmann sparked an urban revolution that would alter the way society understands the very nature of a city. The ramshackle, poorer neighborhoods were demolished, a quarter of a million poor were sent to the outer suburbs. The homes of Victor Hugo's *Les Miserables* were replaced by wide boulevards, opera houses, stylish homes, and department stores. The redesign of downtown Paris represented a new kind of economy, a new society based on leisure, entertainment, consumption, and creative industries.

THE VISUAL REVOLUTION

The printing presses of Paris that for years had churned out radical philosophical and political manifestos now produced a new cultural symbol: the poster. Posters had been around for centuries, but these were different, they were not text-driven, calling for revolution or religious piety, they were image-driven. These posters used silhouettes of beautiful women and stylish men, promoting nightclubs, operas, cafes, and cabarets. This was the new and arresting language of consumerism. It did not need to convince with rhetoric and force of argument, rather it spoke to the wants, desires, and dreams of the Parisian population.

Paris was not just a city of symbols and images; it was quickly becoming an image itself. Real life was becoming objectified, held at a distance. Death, once part of communal life, was now becoming part of the spectacle. Multitudes flocked to the city morgue to view displays of unidentified bodies as death itself became a form of entertainment. Gustave Eiffel's tower had changed Paris, but his creation of the Bon Marché, the very first department store, would change the world. Author Emile Zola would note that these stores operated like religious spaces; worship became window shopping. This new mood of voyeurism spawned the wax museum. Wax museums became the places of worship in the emerging culture of celebrity, as ordinary people could stand within touching distance of replicas of the famous. As wax museums grew in sophistication, whole new visual spaces emerged: museums, dioramas, cycloramas, and panoramas. These media environments prepared the way for the cinema—our dominant form of storytelling today—as the Lumière brothers' first motion picture, *La Sortie de l'Usine Lumière à Lyon*, premiered at a Paris cafe in 1895.

THE TWENTY-FOOT-HIGH WOMAN

So caught up in the thrill of the Exposition of 1889, Paris held another eleven years later. The shift in feel, focus, and narrative could not have been more dramatic. In the former Exposition, the Eiffel Tower dominated. This year another telling centerpiece was created, another manifestation of Leviathan. It was a twenty-foot statue of a young woman dressed in the latest fashions, and it was called *La Parisienne*. The technological wonder of the Eiffel Tower had promised a new kind of utopia. Now within the space of one year, the statue heralded the arrival of the citizen of that promised utopia. The seismic nature of this move cannot be overestimated.

The statue set the tone for the whole Exposition and symbolized what Paris would become, as historian Colin Jones explains:

> It chose to emphasize the pleasures of the senses, and to encourage visitors to think of themselves more as consumers than as citizens . . . The Exposition put the spotlight on the city as the home of the modernist good life, a heady consumerist mix including bright fabrics, haute couture (yet also ready-made clothing), patterned wallpapers, bicycles, cameras, light-bulbs, sewing machines and sundry home comforts.[3]

The statue representing a middle-class, fashionable young woman, was based upon the most famous Parisian woman of the day, the actress Sarah Bernhardt. Bernhardt was known simply as "The Divine Sarah." She was an atheist of Jewish descent, a former high-end prostitute who slept in a coffin and conducted a series of scandalous affairs. Bernhardt's most famous role was to controversially play the male role of Shakespeare's Hamlet. It was a fitting character choice. Many critics have noted that the tragic character of Hamlet represented the first modern character. The poet W. H. Auden once said that "Hamlet lacks faith in God and in himself. Consequently he must define his existence in terms of others."[4] So the twenty-foot statue of the young fashionable woman, modeled on the woman who reinvented herself as Hamlet, perfectly summed up the mood of an age in which people would no longer be defined by the strictures of the past, but who would live with the burdensome freedom of personal reinvention.

GOING MAD WITH EXCITEMENT

Although the Expositions attracted multitudes from all over the world, for the Native Americans of Buffalo Bill's Wild West show, Paris and its Exposition was neither beautiful nor thrilling. The spectacle had deeply disturbed them—and they did not even see the tower of Bernhardt, built the year after they left. Upon completing their tour of all Paris and the Exposition had to offer, in contrast to the wide-eyed crowds, the Indians averted their gaze. They couldn't handle it anymore. One of their chiefs explained to their confused hosts, that they were afraid that they had seen too much in one day. Their chief recommended that they return to their camp lest they go mad with excitement.

THE SOCIETY OF THE SPECTACLE

As we have discussed, the "society of the spectacle" describes a highly visual culture, in which citizens had been reduced to consumers and spectators, in which we were offered a never-ending parade of spectacular media events, which constantly distracted us from mortality, pain, and what it is to be human. In the society of the spectacle, politics is turned into theatre, sex into pornography, religion into consumerism. In the society of the spectacle, reality TV sits next to a terrorist attack broadcast endlessly on the twenty-four-hour news cycle, intermittently interrupted by advertisements for the latest in teeth whitening.

THE PRICE OF ADULTERY

The only antidote to a poison so grand as the myth of Paris is the disappointment of experience. Guy de Maupassant's short story "A

Parisian Affair" surgically dissects the myth of the society of spectacle with brutal flair. De Maupassant's narrative begins with a pretty woman living in the country who dreams of Paris whilst sleeping next to her snoring husband. She had never "known a thing beyond the hideously banal monotony of regularly performed duties, which by all accounts was what happily married life consisted of."[5] For her, Paris is a dream world of escape—the city of lights, *representing the height of all magnificent luxury as well as licentiousness.*"[6] The woman's lusty view of Paris has been cultivated by a steady diet of newspaper gossip, creating in her mind the model of a very different kind of man to her white-collar, small-town, conservative husband. Instead she dreamed of "Men who made the headlines and shone like brilliant comets in the darkness of her sombre sky. She pictured the madly exciting lives they must lead, moving from one den of vice to the next, indulging in never-ending and extraordinarily voluptuous orgies, and practising such complex and sophisticated sex as to defy the imagination. It seemed to her that behind the facades of the houses lining the canyon-like boulevards of the city, some amazing erotic secret must lie."[7]

The woman, no longer able to resist the lure of the city, gripped by a nineteenth-century version of "the fear of missing out," concocts an excuse to travel to Paris. Once arrived, she searches the streets looking for tantalizing scandal and spectacle. She fruitlessly searches the cafes, "Nowhere could she discover the dens of iniquity about which she had dreamed."[8] Her dreams decomposing, she by chance happens upon an aging celebrity writer in one of the new department stores. Throwing aside her usual reserve, she aggressively flirts with him. The writer takes her on a tour of the sights and sounds of Paris. At the theatre, thrillingly, "she was seen by the entire audience, sitting by his side in the first row of the balcony."[9] As the entertainment ends, the writer bids her goodnight. She, however, is determined to cross for the first time into the landscape of adultery and offers to accompany him home. After an awkward and unsatisfying sexual encounter, the woman lies awake in the writer's bed, wondering what she has done. She spends the night staring at the unattractive features of the man who, like her husband, snores and snorts through the night. She continues to stare, repulsed as the man's saliva dribbles down his mouth as he sleeps. She flees home feeling as though

> Something inside her, too, had now been swept away. Through the mud, down to the gutter and finally into the sewer had gone all the refuse of her over-excited imagination. Returning home, the image of Paris swept inexorably clean by the cold light of day filled her exhausted mind, and as she reached her room, sobs broke from her now quite frozen heart.[10]

SOCIAL ISOLATION AND THE COST OF FREEDOM

(Gustave Caillebotte, *Paris Street; Rainy Day*, 1877)

The cost to this new era of freedom and individuality can be seen in an 1877 painting by Impressionist Gustave Caillebotte titled *Paris Street; Rainy Day*. The work shows members of Paris's new urban class crossing a clean and expansive boulevard in the rain. What is striking about Caillebotte's painting is the distance that each walker is from each other. There is no conversation, even between the couples. Each figure in the painting carries above their head an umbrella, which seems to act as an urban shield protecting the walkers not just from the rain but social interaction. The scene is ordered, yet a sense of social dislocation and loneliness haunts the picture. The nineteenth century pioneer of sociology Émile Durkheim argued that the emerging modern culture, whilst raising the standard of living, had also created what he labeled *anomie*, a condition in which major cultural change caused in the individuals moral confusion and a loss of purpose. De Maupassant's story illustrates this understanding of anomie, the woman finds herself a victim of the false promises of the society of the spectacle. A loss of social connection and meaning haunts the freedom of the modern age.

In Émile Zola's 1871 novel *The Kill*, Renée, an upwardly mobile member of France's new urban elite, is traveling through Paris. All around her are sights of the new opulent city. Renée however is no longer entranced by the new city. The beauty of Paris "had made her more acutely aware of the emptiness of her existence. At length she broke her silence with these words, repeated in a tone of muffled anger. 'Oh I'm bored! I'm bored to death.' "[11] Her friends traveling with her in the carriage cannot believe that someone in this city, with such access to so much could be bored. Her friend retorts, "You spend more than a hundred thousand francs a year on your wardrobe, you live in a splendid house . . . Women are jealous of you, and men would give ten years of their lives to kiss the tips of your fingers . . . There is no pleasure you haven't jumped into with both feet."[12] Her male friend now chimes in, questioning the young woman, "And, you're bored! . . . You slay me! . . . But what do you want? What do you dream of?" Renée, herself confused, replies, "What I need is something different, I have no idea what that might be, you understand. But something different, something that's never happened to anyone else, something out of the ordinary, a pleasure of some unfamiliar kind."[13] No longer was satisfaction to be found in duty, responsibility, strong relational ties, but instead in novelty and constant stimulation—an impossible task that creates an addictive downward spiral, generating *ennui*, a frustrated boredom. For the Parisian poet Charles Baudelaire, this was the great threat of the modern world. He proclaimed that this world-weariness was a monster "who is uglier, nastier, more foul! Although he makes no grand gestures, no great noise, He would willingly reduce the earth to ruins. And swallow the world in a yawn; It is Ennui!"[14] *Anomie, ennui*, social isolation, the vapidity of the society of the spectacle. These were the telltale signs of the exhaustion that comes from worshiping idols, the despair that comes from fleeing the face of God. As Psalm 115 tells us of idols,

> Those who make them will be like them,
>   and so will all who trust in them. (v. 8)

The leader ready to bring God's Word must keep her eyes and ears open for these signs of cultural exhaustion. They are the doorways to the human heart.

LEADING IN THE SOCIETY OF THE SPECTACLE

FOR THOSE WHO WISH TO LEAD, INFLUENCE, AND CREATE, THE SOCIETY OF THE SPECTACLE IS ONE OF OUR GREATEST ADVERSARIES. IT ULTIMATELY CREATES SPECTATORS AND CONSUMERS RATHER THAN ACTIVISTS AND CREATORS. IT FUELS DISTRACTION AND PASSIVITY.

Leaders are men and women who can influence a group of people toward a common goal. Their leverage comes from their ability to envision, communicate, and embody a better future. They see something wrong and want to change it. Yet for a group to be motivated they must come to some level of disillusionment with the status quo; they need motivation to change. The difficulty for those of us who are called into leadership in this era, in a society of the spectacle riddled with passive spectatorship and intermittent distraction, is made increasingly difficult.

The society of the spectacle creates passivity among its citizens, a reluctance to initiate, to lead. Instead we are encouraged to view, to consume. We fear committing, worrying that by doing so we will reduce our freedom, cut ourselves off from the myriad of choices that constantly entice us.

The inner workings of the society of the spectacle and its effect on leadership may begin to feel a little overwhelming. However, it's important to realize that this culture of distraction is nothing new—Christianity was born into one. The first-century Roman satirist Juvenal, writing during the period of the early church, complained that Romans had abdicated their responsibility to make a better society and instead were more anxious about "bread and circuses," referring to feasting and the blood sports that were considered entertainment in the Roman Empire. The society of the spectacle is a culture built upon illusion, distraction, and entertainment, which runs from the inevitable storms of human sinfulness, injustice, and brokenness. The society of the spectacle attempts to protect itself from discomfort and pain, like Captain Nemo, by creating a self-contained world of comfort. The Roman culture that Christianity first flourished in was a society of the spectacle. Nothing symbolized the Roman society of the spectacle as much as the blood sports of the Colosseum. The crowds would sit and watch the endless gore and blood.

Yet one day in the arena, the piercing voice of Telemachus rang out, puncturing the day's events with the simple word "Stop!" Tragically, he was killed upon the spot, yet his courageous protest exerted a powerful effect on that day's proceedings: he shamed the emperor into stopping the spectacle. Telemachus's example embodies two important lessons for leadership within a society of spectacle. Firstly, to lead in such a time, one must break from the culture of passivity and spectatorship and be proactive, decide to no longer be slavishly controlled by a culture that pushes us toward passivity. Secondly, when a leader makes this step, there is always a cost. In proactively choosing to stand up for something, you will actively refuse the promises of something else—in our case, the society of the spectacle. Unlike Telemachus, who was never given the chance,

WHEN TODAY'S LEADER REJECTS THE CULTURE OF DISTRACTION, SHE MUST THEN ENCOUNTER THE PAIN AND BROKENNESS THAT WAS PRESENT ALL ALONG— DROWNED OUT BY REALITY TV, SOCIAL NETWORKING,

AND THE CONSTANT HUM OF ADVERTISING. THIS IS PROFOUNDLY COUNTERINTUITIVE, BUT IT IS THE TRUE CALL OF A LEADER.

Reducing your options is particularly difficult for people raised in the society of the spectacle. By stepping into leadership, you refuse to stay within the narrow parameters of contemporary culture and you decide to accept the price of your decision: you choose only one option, and thus negate the seemingly endless possibilities culture appears to offer. Picture a businessman who must choose to invest company money wisely rather than gambling on potentially lucrative but risky deals. Or a professor who must refuse to adopt or teach certain philosophical theories that ultimately deny the divinity of Christ. Your narrow options require your rebellion and may often have unpleasant results. Whilst from a human perspective, particularly when you are young, the future seems like a million different possible permutations or countless parallel universes into which you can step. From God's perspective, however, there is a plan, a purpose, a grand, driving narrative in which you play a role.

LEADERS DO NOT CHOOSE, RATHER THEY RESPOND TO GOD CHOOSING THEM. THUS, THE FIRST RESPONSIVE STEP OF LEADERSHIP IS OF UTMOST IMPORTANCE. IT IS AN ACT OF REBELLION AGAINST THE SOCIETY OF THE SPECTACLE— IT IS TO RELINQUISH A LIFE OF MANY OPTIONS SO THAT YOU CAN RECEIVE GOD'S ONE OPTION.

PART IV

LEADERSHIP IN THE STORM

But Jonah ran away from the Lord and headed for Tarshish.

—JONAH 1:3

SHIPS TO TARSHISH

Jonah's life demonstrates the power of responding to God's call and confronting the sacrifice of one's seemingly unlimited options. We will need to examine this in detail, starting with the beginning of the book. The story of Jonah tells us virtually nothing about the man apart from the name of his father. Instead the narrative begins with God's Word and His call upon Jonah's life. God has a clear mandate for the man: "The word of the Lord came to Jonah son of Amittai: Go to the great city of Nineveh and preach against it, because its wickedness has come up before me" (Jonah 1:1–2).

The Word of God asks that Jonah cease whatever he was doing to take a step into God's plan of redemption for Nineveh. The city of Nineveh, according to the third chapter of Nahum, is wealthy and alluring, the kind of place that ambitious people are drawn to, yet its wealth and charm is built upon injustice and violence. Thus Nineveh is a city that incurs God's wrath:

"I am against you,"
   declares the Lord Almighty,
   "I will lift your skirts over your face.
I will show the nations your nakedness
   and the kingdoms your shame.

I will pelt you with filth,
  I will treat you with contempt
  and make you a spectacle." (Nahum 3:5–6)

A society of the spectacle will be made into a shameful spectacle. God will expose her illusions and distractions, allowing the world to see her sin. To do this He needs a prophet, a leader to communicate His Word of judgment.

IN TIMES OF GREAT UNTRUTH, GOD WILL CALL LEADERS TO BE HIS HERALDS OF TRUTH.

Jonah flees from this task, choosing instead to take the first boat to a city known as Tarshish: "But Jonah ran away from the Lord and headed for Tarshish. He went down to Joppa, where he found a ship bound for that port. After paying the fare, he went aboard and sailed for Tarshish to flee from the Lord" (Jonah 1:3).

The city of Tarshish is not known for its injustice and oppression like Nineveh, but it is a city of wealth and of trade—a cosmopolitan culture that provides Israel with its consumer goodies. Unlike Nineveh, there is an air of the mysterious about Tarshish. Biblical scholars struggle to identify the exact location of this city. Tarshish may have been an exact location that the readers of Jonah would have clearly known about or "it may have not referred to a specific place at all, but may have functioned as a shorthand for something like 'the farther regions.' Or it may have been a very different region they actually knew very little about, but about which they had formed an idealized conception,"[1] writes biblical scholar Richard Mouw.

Psalm 48 describes a judgment, not against the city of Tarshish but against its ships, indicating that these ships represent a symbolic function. They symbolize distant possibilities, a hazy future that one could dream about that promises wealth and prosperity. For Israel they represent a pagan alternative to the rule of God, which in the place of worship offers material satisfaction. Mouw observes that the ships' pagan function is a "means of rebellion against God. They are vessels used to flee from his presence, instruments designed to thwart his will."[2]

THE WORD VS. THE SOCIETY OF THE SPECTACLE

Jonah is thus seemingly caught between two cities, two cultures of evident wealth and power. Yet there is a third element at play: the Word of God. In contrast to the powerful city of Nineveh full of plunder and show, in contrast to the tangible delights and potentials of the ships of Tarshish, stands God's Word. Just as God's Word commanded the universe into being, His Word now comes to Jonah, reshaping him, preparing him for his role in God's unfolding drama. The drama of Jonah's story is not found in his interactions with these great cities, it is found in God's Word. "The whole story is initiated and moved along and shaped by the Word of the Lord, without which there would be no story, no movement, no tension, no flight, and no rescue,"[3] writes Phillip Cary. The Word of God creates and saves. So now, before he can become an instrument of salvation for the people of Nineveh, salvation must come to Jonah.

BEFORE THE LEADER CAN SAVE, HE FIRST MUST BE SAVED. BEFORE HE CAN SPEAK GOD'S WORD, HE MUST ENCOUNTER THE WORD.

Before we can lead others out of the culture of illusions, our illusions must die. As Henry and Richard Blackaby wisely advise in their book *Spiritual Leadership*, "His concern is not to fulfill . . . dreams and goals. . . . His purpose is to turn his people away from their self-centeredness and obsession with temporal, material concerns and to draw them into a relationship with himself so they are his instruments for accomplishing his purposes."[4] The Word of God invites us into the unfolding cosmic drama of which we have always played a part, even without being aware of it. Our childhood experiences, triumphs, and tragedies are all part of God's shaping of our lives, which are, more importantly, about the shaping of His story. When we understand that our lives are not a random collection of experiences but rather a part of God's grand drama we discover that we are gifted by God, blessed with talents and treasures, not for our own ends, but as resources to contribute to His plan to redeem the world by His Word. Leaders then begin to recognize the design and purpose inherent in their lives.

IN THE FRAGMENTARY WORLD OF SENSATION AND SPECTACLE, DECLINING THE GLITZ AND GLAMOUR OF CONSUMERISM ENABLES LEADERS TO SEE COHERENCE IN THEIR EXPERIENCES.

We must not forget how powerfully countercultural this is. Reflecting upon the call of Jonah, Jacques Ellul writes, "When the word intervenes in a situation, it changes that situation. When it comes on a man, it changes that man . . . The word enlists man in an adventure into which he carries all those around him."[5]

THE LEADER'S TASK IN THE VISUAL JUNGLE THAT IS THE SOCIETY OF THE SPECTACLE

IS TO ALLOW HIMSELF TO BE

TRANSFORMED BY THE WORD.

ENCOUNTERING DESTRUCTION

After Jonah boards his ship bound for Tarshish, the Lord intervenes.

> But Jonah ran away from the Lord and headed for Tarshish. He went down to Joppa, where he found a ship bound for that port. After paying the fare, he went aboard and sailed for Tarshish to flee from the Lord.
>
> Then the Lord sent a great wind on the sea, and such a violent storm arose that the ship threatened to break up. All the sailors were afraid and each cried out to his own god. And they threw the cargo into the sea to lighten the ship.
>
> But Jonah had gone below deck, where he lay down and fell into a deep sleep. (Jonah 1:3–5)

Jonah, having bought his way onto the ship headed for Tarshish, retreats beneath deck. The Scriptures make clear that he is in the inner part of the ship. Like Jules Verne's Nemo, Jonah now attempts to flee from the troubles of the world. Yet, there is no comfort to be found in fleeing from the presence and purposes of God.

Jonah going down into the inner part of the ship and falling fast asleep conjures up two images. The first image is of death. In the Hebrew worldview the sea represents death. Jonah going down into the dark hold, under the waterline of the sea, is a metaphor for entering into the world of the dead. In contrast, God's Word brings life. It commands us into activity on behalf of God. Humans were created by God to be His stewards of creation. God's breath brought Adam to life out of the earth. By resisting God's Word, His life-giving breath, Jonah falls into the sleep of death. The ship becomes a coffin, bobbing on the depths. The second image is of immaturity. A grown man sleeping, hiding away from responsibility in the inner part of a ship, to sleep in its comfort, is a reversal of maturity. Humans are born from the womb, we emerge, grow, develop, take upon ourselves responsibility and God's instructions that move us on to maturity.

LEADERS ARE CALLED BY GOD TO MATURE.

Yet here Jonah attempts to reverse this natural progression.

God is not content to have His purposes thwarted, nor is He happy to allow Jonah to slip into metaphorical death or immaturity. While Jonah may feel comfortable and content hidden away in the hull, the ships of Tarshish are dangerous places. The prophet Ezekiel proclaims the spiritual cost associated in the ships of Tarshish when he issues God's judgment against the city of Tyre.

> The ships of Tarshish serve
>   as carriers for your wares.
> You are filled with heavy cargo
>   as you sail the sea.
> Your oarsmen take you
>   out to the high seas.
> But the east wind will break you to pieces
>   far out at sea.
> Your wealth, merchandise and wares,
>   your mariners, sailors and shipwrights,

your merchants and all your soldiers,
   and everyone else on board
will sink into the heart of the sea. (Ezekiel 27:25–27)

God exposes the vulnerability of Tarshish ships by sending a violent storm to do His bidding. God's divine wind makes a mockery of Jonah's plan for escape and his hiding place in the wooden craft. Such man-made protection can do nothing in the face of God's power and omnipotence. A storm is sent and it is sent to destroy. Yet this is a different kind of destruction. The ship to Tarshish will not be destroyed. What will be destroyed, however, is Jonah's attempt to flee God—his effort to, like Captain Nemo, create his own insulated, one-man society in the hull. What is smashed by God's meteorological messenger is Jonah's attempt to keep his options open. Before God's judgment can fall upon Nineveh, Jonah must feel that judgment; he must experience the full effect of the storm so that a foreign, idolatrous but ultimately repentant city may experience grace.

JONAH AND THE SEA

Jonah's boat is wracked by the waves. Phillip Cary writes, "It is as if the world itself is about to break up. The orderly little human world of a ship at sea, so carefully constructed and maintained, is overwhelmed by the vast unruly waters surrounding it on every side. No work of human hand or mind, no technology or skill, is a match for the huge inhuman power of the waters."[6]

This is not the destination point he dreamed of when he planned his escape from the will of God. This was not Tarshish with all its treasures and promises. Jonah had not wanted to be bound by the singular purpose God designed for him, so he ran for the expanse of the open seas. Yet now he is imprisoned. "At this point, all the world Jonah has is this fragile wooden structure borne up by hostile waters and populated by terrified seamen."[7]

The captain found Jonah, still sleeping, and said, "How can you sleep? Get up and call on your god! Maybe he will take notice of us so that we will not perish" (Jonah 1:6). Then the sailors said to each other, "Come, let us cast lots to find out who is responsible for this calamity" (1:7). They cast lots and the lot fell on Jonah. So they asked him, "Tell us, who is responsible for making all this trouble for us? What kind of work do you do? Where do you come from? What is your country? From what people are you?" (1:8). He answered, "I am a Hebrew and I worship the Lord, the God of heaven, who made the sea and the dry land" (1:9). The text continues, saying, "This terrified them and they asked, "What have you done?" (They knew he was running away from the Lord, because he had already told them so)" (1:10).

The urgency of their predicament forces Jonah, a vessel chosen by God, to make a choice. This small group of sailors, travelers, and traders now must form a community. Each calls to his god. However, when faced with the chaos of the deep, which came up and destroyed the world during the flood, these petty, parochial gods are ineffectual. The sailors, who no doubt would have been accustomed to rough passages of open water, see something dangerously different in this storm: they have now exhausted the idols of their respective cultures.

JONAH FINDS HIMSELF
PHYSICALLY AND SPIRITUALLY
IN A STORM. THE STORM

WE CONFRONT IN OUR
CONTEMPORARY MOMENT
PROMISES COMFORT,
ENTERTAINMENT, AND
DISTRACTION. IF WE LOOK
CLOSELY WE SEE THE
UNDERBELLY, THE CHAOS
OF THE DEEP—THE BROKEN
RELATIONSHIPS, THE
ADDICTION OF SUBSTANCE
AND SENSATION, A SOCIETY
WRACKED WITH ANXIETY.

In these confrontations we face a deeply challenging moment that forces us to truly examine our ethics, to take a cold, hard look at how our beliefs and actions truly intersect. Will we simply join in with the herd and run from the storm? Will we offer them distractions, new idols, encased in the language of faith? Or, will we bring them the Word? Will we lead?

THE STORM ON STAGE

In the space of thirty seconds I felt like I had just blown my ministry career. I buried my head in my hands. I could smell the grass. As I sat on the curb, a kid of about twelve from the earlier Chinese congregation circled on his skateboard, staring at me. I could feel the presence of someone behind me, I could see my brother's shoes out of the corner of my eye. "I have ruined it all. There is no going back from that," I said to him.

That Sunday had started like any other. I had my sermon prepared, it was the last song before I was due to go on stage and preach. Then it started to happen again. That heinous emotion sideswiped me like an out-of-control car. The emotion that made you feel like everyone that you loved had burnt everything that you find precious in the world atop a treacherous bonfire. Whilst my stomach was dealing with that feeling, that familiar sensation broke out in my chest and neck, that unwelcoming tightening that slowly crushes you. Then the final phase, that point where everything becomes unbearable, and even the most innocuous of sounds slices through your body. You cannot focus your sight anywhere, human sensation becomes too much. This was not a new experience; it had happened to me before whilst preaching. Each time, somehow, by some gargantuan effort of self-discipline I had pulled through. Afterward I would collapse in the driver's seat of my car, receiving text messages congratulating me on my sermon while tears streamed down my cheeks.

This time however, I reached inside for that strength and came up empty-handed. I looked around for one of my staff or my wife or a confidant to pray for me. Everyone was either too far away or singing with the worship team. Then a person appeared next to me. I had known him for years from my neighborhood. Sadly, he had struggled with schizophrenia. I felt him lean in to whisper in my ear, "You and I are entering psychosis. Can you feel it?" Everything in me wanted to run away. The song ended and I climbed on stage. I began to worry that my legs would not support me. I grabbed one of the stools that the worship band had used and began to speak. My eyes were drawn to the ground like magnets. I could not make eye contact with the congregation. I never use notes, so I had nothing to reference, nothing to remind me of what I wanted to say. I started my sermon, but confusion washed over me.

I quickly realized that I was not making sense. A nervous murmur of laughter broke out; people thought I was trying to be funny. However the silence that followed confirmed that people sensed I was in trouble. The silence was punctured by a baby's cry at the back of the church. The sound cut through me. I could handle it no more. I got up from the stool, mumbled something to the effect that I could not do this anymore, and walked off the stage and out of the church. As I left I could see the looks of confusion, of concern. I could see my leaders exchanging "What on earth do we do now" looks. I had seen people walk out of church upset once or twice. They were people in the congregation who were going through some kind of difficulty. As they left, people looked at each other with sympathetic expressions. However, this was different. We look to our leaders for guidance and stability. When chaos swirls around us, the leader's confidence anchors us. They model the belief that everything will be okay. A ship captain is supposed to ensure everyone else's safety first, then go down with the ship.

What happens when the captain jumps over the starboard bow in the middle of a storm?

THE STORM BENEATH THE SURFACE

The personal storm that overtook me on stage that day had been brewing for some time. Yet on the surface everything looked great. The markers of Christian leadership success were in my favor. I had recently taken the senior leadership role of my church. I was well known in Christian circles in Australia. I was receiving more speaking requests than I could fulfill. I wrote a popular blog. I had just released my second book, and I had a book tour lined up that would send me to three continents. With a design studio I had created a unique online novel and photographic project. I was a regular on radio shows, discussing the intersection between faith and culture. In fact, culture was what I was all about. I was sought out to comment upon, dissect, and interpret culture—to understand how faith can survive in the midst of our cultural storm. Those who struggled to deal with the pace of cultural change used me as a resource to guide them through the fog. Yet underneath it all I was engaged in an all-consuming battle.

A week before I had walked off stage, my personal storm had overtaken me. I was in another city for a speaking engagement. I was alone in a hotel room, away from all the familiarity of home, when I experienced an even more intense version of what would soon be hitting me on stage. A few days later I was sitting in a psychiatrist's office. I was told that I had suffered what is called a "mixed episode," something people with bipolar disorder encounter, in which the sufferer experiences both depression and mania simultaneously.

When I would experience the beginnings of a manic mood, I would feel on top of the world. I had boundless energy. I could write for twelve hours, pouring out ideas. I could speak at break-neck pace, linking disparate topics. I was funny, charming, excit-able. I would pace around my office or my house with fast music pumping, with themes and ideas firing in my head. My mind was like a Ferrari engine firing on all cylinders. I would struggle to sleep. I would fall in love with the world, weeping with joy at a piece of music or the shade of green in the leaves of a tree. I could conquer anything. I was unbeatable.

Then the exhaustion would kick in. The looks on other people's faces when I was talking too fast or when they could no longer fol-low my train of thought would alert me to the fact that something was wrong. The sensation of living would become too painful. The trees that were once so beautiful now became too much, the music that was sending me into euphoria would now become unbear-able. The brilliant ideas that I had generated, the world-changing schemes and plans appeared farcical in the cold, hard light of the next day. Then would come the low.

At first the low could even be comforting, a respite from the tiring high. The desire to see others would fade. My mind would become foggy. My body would slow down. I would be overcome with tiredness. Whereas during the high, the world sparkled in brilliant color, everything now looked one dimensional and mono-chromatic. At first I would want to hide. Then I would start to hate the world. I would become sickened, negative, and cynical. I would wish that the deep, dark recesses would rise and sweep away this horror of a planet. I would fall away into an abyss of self-hatred, despair, and darkness. I would sink down into the deep, chaotic sea. Christian leadership is a difficult task. However, having to lead with the roller coaster of emotions brought on by bipolarity seemed desperately unfair.

LEADERSHIP AND THE FAIRNESS OF GOD

In some ways Jonah's reticence to follow God's call is perfectly understandable. As Scripture provides very little background to his life, we can only speculate at his circumstances. After receiving his charge from God, Jonah continues to Joppa. Joppa was a port city with a vibrant multicultural population. It was Israel's receiving point for imports from other nations. With its large percentage of Gentiles, it would have been a very different entity to the spiritual stronghold of Jerusalem. Life in Jerusalem moved around the temple, regulated around the worship of Yahweh. Port cities like Joppa were built upon goods, trade, and money. In trading cities, one can feel the pull of faraway places, the lure of potential riches and the tug of adventure. They are filled with opportunists, entrepreneurs, and self-made people. In such a place it would have been easy for Jonah to compare his lot with others. Why must *he* be called to preach to the Ninevites?

Comparing your lot with your neighbor became a keystone of modern culture. As the western world moved away from monarchies to a democratic view of society based upon fairness and equality, this sense of comparison would only grow. As the West moved toward the ideal of classlessness, society began to believe that everyone should receive the same opportunities and enjoy the same privileges. This new society generated a fresh understanding of justice, one that looked to natural law to devise ideas of "rights," such as the right to happiness, property, and freedom that should apply to every individual. Alongside these developments, modern consumerism would offer an impressive host of goods, services, and luxuries, once only affordable to the rich, solidifying the expectation that glamour, power, and ease are attainable by anyone, rather than exclusively to the aristocracy. Rampant consumerism breeds a sense of social competition, where we are encouraged to keep up with the lifestyles of our friends and neighbors. To get ahead, we increase our consumption in order to reach the next level of status. Comparison, competition, and status anxiety marked the modern consciousness.

So when God then asks something of us it can be jarring. People who live in democracy are not used to being told what to do by a king, someone who has the authority to issue a nonnegotiable decree. Our culture of the West is based upon a rejection of the divine right of kings, but God remains on His throne. The idea that God would interrupt our agenda, our will, and seemingly trample upon our rights by asking us to do something—anything—is deeply troubling to the contemporary person. It is an intrusion on our autonomy. When God asks us to do something that endangers our social status, it is equally as upsetting. Our default position of comparison will only make the process worse. The fact remains: God's justice does not simply mirror our culture's idea of justice.

THE LEADER MUST SURRENDER THEIR PERSONAL AND CULTURAL CONSTRUCTS OF FAIRNESS, SUBMITTING AND SURRENDERING TO GOD'S JUSTICE.

IF WE OBEY GOD, WE MUST DISOBEY OURSELVES

While Jonah didn't live in a modern day democracy, he was still terrified of God's call. It conflicted with his autonomy. Jonah is running away from God, from his identity as part of God's people. Now, in the midst of the storm, his hand is forced. When the crew inquire about his identity, he must reply. He is a Hebrew. He is not from the nations. He is part of the people called apart by God to witness to His majesty and righteousness. You can almost feel the sense of holy resignation in Jonah's reply. "I am a Hebrew and worship the Lord, the God of heaven, who made the sea and the dry land." Jonah's reply is both gospel and repentance. The crew now know the name of the only being in the universe who can save them. Jonah is now delivering the Word. And with the delivery of the Word comes life. Jonah is now roused from his slumber in the hold. The ship that is about to break up and the crew that are about to be buried in the watery underworld now can sense the possibility of life. Like all believers, Jonah is adept at talking himself out of God's command. Obedience for Jonah is optional. However the sailors, in their blunt paganism, can see through this guise. They understand instantly that their present danger is due to some disobedience or sin on Jonah's part. There is a great lesson here for us.

In *Moby Dick*, Herman Melville includes a chapter in which a sea dog of an old pastor in a church built for sailors delivers a sermon on the book of Jonah. The pastor preaching from his strange lectern shaped like a boat loudly thunders, "What a pregnant lesson to us is this prophet! . . . All the things that God would have us do are hard for us,"[8] says the preacher reminding the audience of the cost of following God. The hardest thing in following God, according to this strange prophetic chaplain of the sea, is rooted in the truth that "If we obey God, we must disobey ourselves."[9] God asked Jonah to obey. This meant that Jonah had to disobey himself, to cast aside his agenda, his dream.

THE HEBREW IN THE HOLD

JONAH'S SELF-DISOBEDIENCE— HIS *NO* TO SELF—AWAKENS THE LEADER, THE PROPHET, THE INFLUENCER WITHIN HIM.

When the storm comes, it is the cry of the pagan crew who awakens the previously reluctant man of God. Their salvation is dependent upon his waking. Jonah's story carries great significance for us today:

> For in the last resort Jonah can refuse to admit his guilt. He can continue to outface God and say no. If he does, he knows what the result will be. The vessel will go down with all hands. This is our situation. If in the common danger suspended over the world Christians shun their function, if Christians who have received inestimable grace refuse to take it to the world, then the rest, pagans, non-Christians, those who man the enterprises in which we are engaged, will perish. Christians have to realize that they hold in their hands the fate of their companions.[10]

Heavy words indeed from Jacques Ellul, a sociologist and lay leader in the Reformed Church of France during World War II. Jonah's story carried particular significance for him. The collaborationist French government working with the Nazis had passed laws requiring Jews to identify themselves, which led to their eventual transportation to concentration camps. The question of whether he would continue like Jonah to comfortably "slumber" in the hold was very real to Ellul. A cultural storm had overtaken his nation, which would have life-and-death consequences for his Jewish fellow citizens. Reflecting upon how God treats Jonah, Ellul wrote, "He confronts Jonah with his responsibilities. He impales him on the horns of his dilemma. According to scripture this is often God's way with man. He forces on him an ineluctable choice . . . He does not manipulate him like a puppet. On the contrary, he appeals to the high point of his freedom, to choice. But this is a choice of difficult alternatives."[11] Ellul came to realize that

IN THE WORST CULTURAL STORM, THERE IS ALWAYS THE KERNEL OF GOOD NEWS, A HEBREW IN THE HOLD, A PERSON OF GOD READY TO BE AWOKEN.

In choosing to obey God in the midst of the Third Reich, Ellul risked his life saving Jews from the gas chambers.

FOR LEADERSHIP TO BE AWOKEN, THE MODERN MYTH THAT, LIKE NEMO, WE CAN HIDE AWAY FROM THE STORMS OF LIFE IN COMFORT MUST BE CAST ASIDE.

PART V

WHEN THE LEADER JUMPS OVERBOARD

I would annex the planets if I could.

—**CECIL RHODES,** a nineteenth-century African explorer

BEHIND THOSE EYES

Augusta Webb, commenting on her friend Henry Morton Stanley, would say: "He had . . . the most extraordinary and wonderful eyes I had ever seen. They were like small pools of grey fire, but the least provocation turned them into grey lightning."[1]

Was it the grey blue eyes? Eyes that were at once entrancing yet cold and distant, eyes that seemed to reflect the allure and the wild fear of the endless African savannah in which his fame had been hewn. Was it the scent of the exotic that lingered in a room after he left, long after the stories of adventure had ended, the fire had cooled in the hearth, and the dignitaries had departed for home? Was it that he represented a new specimen of man, one of the first global citizens in a world shrunken by technology, who could traverse the globe in a justice-fueled quest to eradicate the scourge of slavery? Or, maybe he was a throwback to an older kind of man, a man of valor who was not simply willing to effect change through legislation and pamphlets but who waded into the world's problems, boots first? Was it his passion to proclaim the gospel amongst people and places that were not plotted on any Western map? Could it be as simple as the fact that in any era, a man who leads from the front into wild and dangerous places is simply magnetic? Either way Henry Morton Stanley caught the world's attention.

A NEW KIND OF INFLUENCER IS BORN

The city of spectacle was about to engineer a storm of publicity that would capture the public's attention. A society of the spectacle needed spectacular heroes. The world had followed with fascination the exploits of David Livingstone, Scottish missionary and doctor. Livingstone had left behind his home in Britain to evangelize and explore the center of Africa. Exploring Africa was nothing new for Europeans, but something about Livingstone's personality and task resonated with a public hungry for heroes. Livingstone's desire to see slavery eradicated from Africa only added to his popularity.

By the nineteenth century, William Wilberforce's revolution against slavery was becoming the public cause of the day. Whilst the European powers on the whole had turned from the practice, Islamic Afro-Arabic and North African slave traders had continued buying and selling humans as they had for over a millennium. By the second half of the nineteenth century this trade had reached incredible proportions, with up to 90 percent of some Central African people groups sold into slavery. This cause, when allied with the advances wrought by the industrial age such as the steam train and the emerging technology of the telegraph, ensured that reports and letters could be fed back to a public hungry for exotic stories of adventure and justice. Then, silence. David Livingstone, reporting from the edge of the world, seemed to fall off of it.

For six years no news came, and many feared that somewhere in the African interior that the good doctor had finally met the Great Physician in person. Taking up the challenge to find Livingstone, the twenty-eight-year-old Stanley, at the time working as a journalist, broke the rules of impartial reporting and inserted himself squarely front and center of the story. Stanley took off with over two hundred porters, as well equipped as one could be for the challenges of Africa. The stage was set. The hero was ready to enter the drama.

DR. LIVINGSTONE, I PRESUME?

Nine months after landing in Africa, Stanley would finally find the doctor. The event would be recounted to the world in Stanley's bestselling book, *How I Found Livingstone.* Stanley's retelling uses a certain emotional theatricality. Upon finally finding the village in which Livingstone was staying, Stanley "did that which I thought was most dignified. I pushed back the crowds, and, passing from the rear, walked down a living avenue of people, until I came in front of the semicircle of Arabs, before which stood the 'white man with the grey beard.' "[2] The scene is now set for the climax of his journey. "As I advanced slowly towards him I noticed he was pale, that he looked wearied . . . I would have run to him, only I was a coward in the presence of such a mob—would have embraced him, but I did not know how he would receive me; so I did what moral cowardice and false pride suggested was the best thing,"[3] which was to deliver one of the most memorable first greetings in the history of the English language. Stanley took off his hat, and uttered, " 'Dr. Livingstone, I presume?' 'Yes,' said he, with a kind smile, lifting his cap slightly. I replace my hat on my head, and he puts on his cap, and we both grasp hands, and I then say aloud: 'I thank God, Doctor, I have been permitted to see you.' He answered, 'I feel thankful that I am here to welcome you.' "[4] Stanley had now not only entered the aura of Livingstone's person but also his fame. The two traveled together for some time before parting ways. Stanley would unsuccessfully attempt to persuade Livingstone to return to Britain with him. Livingstone would never see home again; two years later he would die on African soil. Stanley would return from Africa a bona fide media star.

Stanley had claimed that he arrived in Africa a virtual heathen, his meeting with the saintly Livingstone stoking the flames of faith that laid dormant within. In his writings and public appearances he spoke of his desire to leave an evangelistic legacy on the African continent, wishing that he would be "selected . . . in opening up Africa to the shining light of Christianity!"[5] Yet judging by his actions, his quest for adventure and personal glory motivated him much more powerfully than preaching the gospel.

BEHIND THE PR

Stanley's personal transformation was now complete. The public now viewed Stanley as the epitome of the African explorer. Whilst the African explorer seemingly dealt in the trade of maps and uncharted territory, their real occupation was in the communication of daring experiences, lived through and communicated as if their lives were straight from the page of a novel. But finding Livingstone was now not enough, and the papers again sent Stanley back to Africa under the pretense of exploring the course of the Congo River. Yet on this expedition Stanley would generate the wrong kind of news.

The man who had come to free Africans from the tyranny of slavery, to open Africa up to the light of Christianity, approached the inhabitants of Bumbire Island on Lake Victoria. He had arrived and had safely positioned his boat fifty yards from the shoreline. At this distance Stanley and his men were out of the range of the locals armed with arrows and spears. All the island's residents could do was to shout and scream in an attempt to repel the foreign invaders. Stanley's previous attempt to land on the island resulted in a minor skirmish that left the explorer humiliated and indignant. The indignation brewed inside of him, turning into vengeance. This vengeance exploded into a volley of gunfire. The fact that neither Stanley nor any of his party were in any danger in their boats did not dissuade them from the use of deadly force. To Stanley, these were not tribal people simply trying to protect their island from potentially dangerous visitors. Their screams and war cries were direct insults, a cacophony of mockery, a personal affront. The residents of Bumbire Island paid a terrible price for their "mocking" as dozens of bodies now lay dead upon shore. The personal storm that had been brewing inside of Henry Morton Stanley was now raging. This young, celebrated leader who had seen it as his mission to bring liberty from injustice and to open up the continent to the gospel had only brought misery and death.

Most who clamor for fame know that it is a fleeting commodity. It must be massaged, tended, and nurtured. With the skill of a contemporary public relations guru, Stanley had built his "personal brand." He networked, created content, worked the media, got on the speaking circuit, and was fast becoming known as Africa's greatest explorer. Yet his actions on the ground, particularly the massacre on Bumbire Island began to cause a media storm in Britain. The image of the earnest, brave explorer and heir to Livingstone's evangelistic crown began to smash into the reality of a man who operated more like a rogue warlord. Stanley's insistence that he had come to free Africans from slavery seemed at complete odds with his boasts of wiping out whole African towns and villages. Reading his reports closely, Stanley's entourage of porters and guides appear more like an army, carrying a small arsenal—one that included a new weapon that ended the lives of a whole generation of young men in the muddy trenches of World War I: the maxim machine gun.

Actual missionaries on the ground seemed to have a very different view of Stanley's legacy than the one he had forged in the media. The African-American missionary George Washington Williams seemed to embody everything that Stanley was not. His impressions of the "great explorer" veer wildly from Stanley's own books: "Far from being a great hero, Stanley had been a tyrant. His name produces a shudder among this simple folk when mentioned; they remember his broken promises, his copious profanity, his hot temper, his heavy blows, his severe and rigorous measures, by which they were robbed of their lands."[6]

Those robbed of their lands gave Stanley a name in their local language of Kongo, *Bula Matari*—the breaker of rocks, a mocking reference to his cruelty. His fellow explorer Richard Francis Burton bluntly reported that Stanley shoots Africans with little thought. If his brutal explorations were not damaging enough to the people of central Africa, worse was to come. The man who had come to free Africans would become embroiled with King Leopold, the Belgian monarch who, wishing to compete with his fellow European powers, would use Stanley's explorations to acquire his own colony: the Belgian Congo. Stanley would be tied to the legacy of one of history's most murderous colonial regimes.

The brutal heritage of Stanley and King Leopold also intersected with Paris. There was a dark underbelly to the society of the spectacle. One of the most popular things to do at the Exposition was to enjoy the new bicycles on sale. The nineteenth century's growing taste for cycling saw the world's demand for rubber tires boom. Visitors could also visit the Congo Village, a human zoo, in which Westerners could stare at poor Congolese abducted by their Belgian colonial masters. There was a direct link between the cycles on sale and the Congo Village. The jungles of the Congo were filled with rubber. One of history's most brutal explorations would see the colonial authorities put the people of the Congo to the dangerous and difficult work of extracting the resource from the rubber trees deep within the jungle. The price of refusing such work was death.

To prove that the necessary executions had been carried out, the African soldiers in the employ of the colonial authorities were required to provide their employers with the hands and feet of those whom they had murdered. Men, women, and children were not spared from this barbaric practice. One of the most heartbreaking records of this horror is the photo of a Congolese man Nsala sitting on the porch of his home, staring at a severed hand and foot that once belonged to his five-year-old daughter; it's said that this was the price for not fulfilling her quota of rubber. The oppression made King Leopold incredibly wealthy. It also tied Stanley to one of history's worst genocides with a death toll of up to ten million Congolese, greater than what would soon follow in World War I. Despite his publicized noble intentions, Stanley's incursion into the Congo delta would set the foundation for a cataclysmic history of oppression, exploitation, and war. The troubles of the Congo would last well into our day. Between the 1990s and the year 2000, up to five million would perish in the region in what has been called the Great War of Africa, an ongoing legacy of the Congo's colonial past.

REAL MEN AND MUSCULAR CHRISTIANITY

As European culture became more stable and as the consumer society grew, a sense of pervading anxiety developed and masculinity was being diminished. An 1841 cartoon in the popular *Punch* magazine features a man standing before an array of beautifying products, paralyzed by his direction in life. The whole of European culture seemed to be confused over the role of the male. "A new time seemed to demand new models, new identities, and it was true that men appeared to be overwhelmed by the demands placed on them,"[7] writes historian Philipp Blom. The nineteenth-century philosopher Thomas Carlyle would famously proclaim that "the history of the world is but the biography of great men," proposing a rediscovery of the tradition of the hero, asserting that history was pushed forward by great men of glory and destiny. All of this was good in theory, but how was one to be a hero or a great man during the industrial revolution, in a culture that was stabilizing and progressing? "Uncivilized" Africa became viewed as an arena in which "civilized" men, hungry for the heroic, could reconnect with a sense of masculinity and meaning.

For those who did not have the gall or the means to head off to faraway lands, they could at least live vicariously through them in the media, as many did through men like Livingstone and Stanley. This code of heroic masculinity was even promoted by the church. Concerned by what he saw as the feminization of society, the Reverend Charles Kingsley proposed what he called "muscular" Christianity, a synthesis of traditional Greek ideals of heroic masculinity, physical fitness (in particular, bodybuilding), and Darwinism. Stanley, driving a path through the African jungle, bringing both gospel and guns, seemed to embody the spirit of muscular Christianity. With all his might he determined to be one of the "great men" that Kingsley and Carlyle called for. He was playing a part in the society of the spectacle, molding a public persona around props of masculinity and heroism. Yet within him pain, insecurity, ambition, and sin swirled, ready to erupt. Traditionally, Christianity's belief that "all have sinned and fall short of the glory of God" (Romans 3:23) had offered an honest assessment of the darkness that resides within the human heart. The Dutch politician and theologian Abraham Kuyper noted that this baseline starting point, that all humans have sinned, created a radical equality. He wrote that "all men or women, rich or poor, weak or strong, dull or talented, as creatures of God, and as lost sinners, have no claim whatsoever to lord over one another."[8] Yet as the Christian story was increasingly marginalized and as the society of the spectacle began to dominate the social consciousness, the old pagan temptations returned. Kuyper had noted that in the pagan worldview "a divine superiority is exhibited,"[9] which gives way to hero-worship. No longer is the inner heart work of God's redeeming and saving love needed. All that is needed is to create a glorious outer facade. To, in short, be a spectacular participant in the society of the spectacle. Writing when Christianity still shaped the dominant worldview of the West, the

German medieval writer Thomas à Kempis taught that "it is good for us to encounter troubles and adversities from time to time, for trouble often compels a man to search his own heart. It reminds him that he is an exile here, and that he can put his trust in nothing in this world . . . A man should therefore place such complete trust in God that he has no need of comfort from men."[10] Yet when trouble comes to us in our society of the spectacle, which encourages an exterior life dependent upon the audience and affirmation of others, without God we have no way of holding back the darkness within. We have no shelter against the storms within our souls.

YOU NEED TO HAVE A QUIET LIFE

Sitting in the psychiatrist's office, my only wish was for the mixed episodes that I was experiencing to stop. As we began to talk about treatment, I could not help wondering how the increasing demands that God was placing upon my life would fit with my condition. I had been engaged in constant ministry for fifteen years. All of my ministry had been involved in the breaking of new ground. Living out the organic values was meant to be an alternative to the workaholism of the mechanical values. Yet I was utterly exhausted. I was struggling to keep my head above water. I had accrued a public profile, the markers of Christian social success surrounded me; yet when the storms hit, they are of no use.

The psychiatrist told me that it was essential that I live a quiet life. As the words came out of his mouth, I was trying to reconcile them with the realities of leadership and ministry. He told me that I needed plenty of sleep. I had to keep a routine and a schedule, to avoid unfamiliar situations and places that were overstimulating and stressful.

My wife's father had just passed away after battling a rare and unforgiving illness. My wife was spent, exhausted from grief whilst caring for our very busy two-year-old daughter. Plus, she was expecting again. As we drove to the obstetrician's office for the first scan, my wife and I decided that we were not concerned whether we had a boy or a girl. I only had two requests of God. First, that the baby was healthy. The second request had formed in my mind a few days earlier. I knew we were pregnant, I was trying to figure out how I was meant to stem these mixed episodes, to feel well again. I drove past a very stressed-looking mother, pushing her twins along in a pram—and said, "God please do not give us twins."

As my wife lay back on the bed, the obstetrician passed the sonar device across her belly. My wife joked that she hoped it was not twins. "Wish again," the obstetrician replied. "*It's twins.*"

I would not swap my twin boys, Hudson and Billy, for anything. However I have to say that the first year of their life pushed me to my limit. It was hard enough putting up with constant work, no social life or downtime, two hours of sleep a night, an exhausted wife, a daughter starved for attention; doing all of this whilst finishing a book, running a growing ministry, and taking a church through a change of management was incredibly challenging. Being asked by God to do all of this, however, while battling bipolarity, felt downright criminal. I was told that for my own health I make it an absolute priority to have a quiet life, and here I was under the most incredible and unrelenting pressure. The effects of the bipolarity refused to let up, the mixed episodes continued to rear their ugly heads.

The only respite I had during this time was when I visited the bathroom. For a few minutes I had those precious moments alone. I would pull out my phone and look at Facebook or Twitter. In moments like that, a kind of lens comes over your eyes, and you evaluate your life by viewing the lives of others around you. *Why did God ask me to do this and not others?* Yet God was still calling me to obey Him. By obeying Him, I was denying myself the rest I felt I deserved and was stepping into His kingdom reality. The book of

Hebrews tells us,

> Endure hardship as discipline; God is treating you as his
> children. For what children are not disciplined by their father?
> If you are not disciplined—and everyone undergoes disci-
> pline—then you are not legitimate, not true sons and daughters
> at all. Moreover, we have all had human fathers who disciplined
> us and we respected them for it. How much more should we
> submit to the Father of spirits and live! They disciplined us
> for a little while as they thought best; but God disciplines us
> for our good, in order that we may share in his holiness. No
> discipline seems pleasant at the time, but painful. Later on,
> however, it produces a harvest of righteousness and peace for
> those who have been trained by it.
>
> Therefore, strengthen your feeble arms and weak knees.
> "Make level paths for your feet," so that the lame may not be
> disabled, but rather healed. (Hebrews 12:7–13)

I was being asked to see the challenge and hardship that I was
facing as discipline. Hebrews challenges us to reframe our suffering
as something that "strengthens our feeble arms and weak knees."
God allows strengthening so that others, particularly the downtrod-
den, may not be defeated, that those who are broken can be healed.
Scripture was encouraging me to see the personal storm that I was
enduring as linked to the healing of others and reminding me that
I'm not the locus of authority in my own life. Such recognition creates the space in which we are remade and reshaped in His image.
I began to realize that God was far more interested in reshaping me
and strengthening me in those private moments than He was in my
public ministry. Culture tells us, however, that it is the public where
heroic leaders are made.

THE HERO

(Gustave Doré, *Destruction of Leviathan*, 1865)

The Greek myth of Prometheus, who stole fire from the gods thus kick-starting human civilization, is the classic hero story. However, the idea of the hero can be traced back to cultures older than the Greek. The tradition of the hero is first found in the myths of the cultures that surrounded the Hebrews. In particular, in a type of battle that scholars call the *Chaoskampf*—a struggle with chaos. In the Babylonian myths, the hero is the storm god Marduk who battles the sea monster god Tiamat. Tiamat is the representation of primordial chaos and disorder. The Babylonian myth the *Enuma Elish* says that she,

> Gave birth to monster snakes, . . .
> fierce dragons, . . .
> serpents, dragons, hairy hero-men, . . .
> mighty demons, fish men, bull men.[11]

The creatures that Tiamat brings into the world are mutations that betray the natural order of the world. They symbolize the monstrous, which frightens us because it represents a dislocation of how the world should be. Marduk battles Tiamat in the epic showdown that anticipates every subsequent epic showdown. At the apex of their battle, Marduk sends a storm wind at Tiamat that ultimately defeats her. With the scent of blood now in his nostrils, Marduk creates the world as we know it by mutilating her body. Marduk through this process establishes Babylon as his base and the center of the universe. The religious implications of this story are clear. To establish our culture of order, chaos must be defeated by power and violence. According to this ideology, our culture, cities, and civilizations are dependent upon our heroes. Our understanding of leadership is markedly shaped by the myth of the hero, the idea that through sheer effort and determination we can reshape reality. The myth of the hero tells us that dynamic, charismatic, and glorious individuals can heal cultures through their personal guile, skill, and glory.

Stanley's journey into Africa to bring "civilization" to "uncivilized Africa" fits the model of the hero, the great man, wading into primal chaos, and through strength and power establishing order. However, chaos can return. This is the message of the ancient Babylonian myths. After she is defeated and mutilated, Tiamat is still not truly gone. As Timothy Beal claims:

Marduk's defeat of Tiamat in the story may appear to be final. Yet on a deeper level there is a lurking sense that the watery monster of primordial chaos might stir and rage out of control yet again if not continually kept under Marduk's lordly control. Tiamat is killed but might not stay that way. Living on the (undead?) slaughtered body of the chaos god who bore you produces at least a little anxiety. In the ancient world, as in the modern monster tale, it is difficult to keep a good monster down. They have a tendency to reawaken, reassemble their dismembered parts, and return for a sequel.[12]

Thus a feeling pervades our world that chaos could overtake us again. This is a foundational element of the stories that shape our contemporary myths. Ordinary people turned into zombies, Voldemort quietly building his army of Death Eaters, Anakin turning to the dark side of the force. We fear that something, or someone, will reinvoke the chaos. The book of Job warns that the Bible's chaos monster, Leviathan, is not easily subdued: "Can you pull in Leviathan with a fishhook or tie down its tongue with a rope? . . . If you lay a hand on it, you will remember the struggle and never do it again! Any hope of subduing it is false; the mere sight of it is overpowering" (Job 41:1, 8–9).

The Joker in Christopher Nolan's *The Dark Knight* gives the mission statement of the chaos monster, "Introduce a little anarchy. Upset the established order, and everything becomes chaos. I'm an agent of chaos."[13] To contain this anarchy, for Gotham City to survive, it needs Batman. The logic seemingly tells us that we need a hero. After the villain is vanquished, chaos is defeated and order restored. The bloodied hero returns to the relieved city's adulation, then rides off into the sunset having won the girl. Yet there is a problem. Whilst the hero is desirable to women, he is not marriage material. His attractiveness comes from the fact that he cannot be domesticated. He cannot fit into normal society. Batman is divided;

Bruce Wayne is created so that he can participate in normal society. Why? Because there is a chaos monster within the hero. Thus, our heroes are cops who don't play by the book, superheroes who struggle to contain their super power, vigilantes who fight and hunt for good. Harry Potter is mysteriously connected to Voldemort; Dexter the serial killer uses his lust for blood for good. The Babylonian myth tells us that Tiamat gives birth to "hairy hero-men." The hero is connected to the chaos monster. He uses violent winds and storms to kill the sea beast, and chaos seemingly kills chaos. Violence defeats violence.

As a result, we tolerate the dangerous presence of pandemonium within the hero. We believe that to kill chaos monsters, you need a little chaos monster in you. We put up with the quirks, the individualism, or even the corruption of the great men. Yet, this individualism, this brokenness, is ominous. The hero, like the leader with unresolved issues, poses a threat. Hugo writes,

> A lot of men have a secret monster like this, an ache that they feed, a dragon that gnaws away at them, a despair that haunts their nights. Such a man looks like any other, comes and goes. You do not know that he has a frightening parasitic pain inside him with a thousand teeth, living inside the miserable wretch and killing him, for he is dying of it. You do not know that this man is a bottomless pit. One where the water is still, but deep. From time to time, a disturbance no one can fathom shows on the surface. A mysterious wrinkle puckers up, then vanishes, then reappears; a bubble of air rises and bursts. It is not much, but it is terrifying. It is the unknown beast breathing.[14]

It was this unknown beast within Stanley that would cause the hero to turn into a chaos monster.

HEART OF DARKNESS

To understand Stanley, we must dig behind his own carefully crafted public persona. As the backlash against the massacre at Bumbire Island gained traction in the media, people began to ask other questions. Why did his American accent seem to fade in and out? Why did facts in his stories seem to not add up? Why did rumors persist about his origins and real name? The answer was simple. Henry Morton Stanley was not Henry Morton Stanley. Stanley's birth certificate read John Rowlands—"bastard." His first language was not English, it was Welsh. His father abandoned him, and his mother was most likely a prostitute. After his guardian uncle dropped dead, he was turned over to his small Welsh town's poorhouse. Life there was brutal, filled with sexual abuse. This traumatic childhood undoubtedly contributed to Stanley's sense of life's injustice and fueled his desire to reinvent himself. He may have been able to present himself to the world as a capable, charismatic person, but the monster inside was lurking.

Before his travels in Africa, one moment sums up Stanley's approach to life. Whilst working as a journalist in what is today Iran, he visited the pre-Roman ruins at Persepolis. Not content to simply peruse the ruins, Stanley scratched his name into the ancient rock, this drive for recognition still visible today. This act, this powerful desire to have his name known is key to understanding Stanley. The ancient Greeks spoke of *Thumos*, the powerful inner drive for recognition; in excess this drive would turn into vengeance. "It was almost as if vengeance were the force driving him across the continent,"[15] reflects Adam Hochschild. Joseph Conrad, the Polish writer who himself traveled to the Congo, saw something prophetic in what was occurring in the Belgian Congo through men like Stanley. Conrad noted that the vengeance wreaked upon local African people illustrated a barbarism deep within the European heart.

Many believe that Joseph Conrad's short novel *Heart of Darkness* was based upon Stanley's life. In the novel the narrator, Marlow, recounts his journey into Africa to make contact with the European trader Kurtz. Kurtz left for Africa as an artist and aspiring leader, as well as author of a pamphlet promoting the civilizing of Africa. Upon finding Kurtz at his remote trading station, Marlow discovers that he has reinvented himself as a tribal warlord. Kurtz's hut is surrounded by skulls. Worshiped as a god by the locals, he rules with a violent hand. Away from the "civilizing" structure and conventions of Europe, men like Kurtz or Stanley, when confronted with the lawlessness of colonial oppression, were overrun with their own personal demons. Whilst technology and progress had improved the standard of living for Westerners, there was an inner poverty in the Western heart. Conrad wrote of Kurtz, "The wilderness whispered to him things about himself that he did not know, things of which he had no conception till he took counsel with this great solitude—and the whisper had proved irresistibly fascinating. It echoed loudly within him because he was hollow at the core."[16]

The colonial rulers of the Belgian Congo erected a statue celebrating Stanley's legacy in the capital city of Kinshasa, which grew out of the trading station that he established. During an uprising in the 1970s, the statue was knocked to the ground by angry Congolese. To this day it remains prostrate. In a piece of irony, his feet are removed from his body, just as the hands and feet were removed from the victims of the rubber trade. If you look closely, where the feet have broken away from the body, you can see that the statue, like the man himself, was hollow to the core.

VAMPIRIC FAME AND INFLUENCE

With his pith helmet, mustache, and African porters in tow, Stanley could appear more as a cliché of an antiquated mode of leadership, yet there was something radically new about his actions. Stanley would anticipate the age of social networking and self-promotion. Hochschild explores the interplay between the emerging fields of media and fame that seem to drive Stanley's actions: "Pre-electronic though they were, Stanley's books were multi-media productions. With every step he took in Africa, Stanley planned how to tell the story once he got home. He was always sculpting the details of his own celebrity."[17] Anticipating our own age in that many view everyday life experiences as moments to be broadcast across the platforms of social networking, Stanley is aware that each step that he takes, each encounter, every exotic experience, can be transmitted to a waiting audience.

Henry Morton Stanley was the product of a society that now focused upon outer experience and sensation, which repositioned leadership and influence away from the discipline of inner growth and character, turning it into celebrity. Shakespeare in his play *The Twelfth Night* wrote, "Some are born great, some achieve greatness and some have greatness thrust upon 'em."[18] Reflecting upon this quote centuries later Daniel J. Boorstin would cynically quip, "It never occurred to him to mention those who hired public relations experts and press secretaries to make themselves look great."[19] Boorstin was marking a profound change in how our culture views leadership and influence, a shift precipitated by our age of the image; we have gone from a culture in which leadership was rooted in positional power, acts of achievement, and strength of character, to one that sees leadership as the careful manipulation of imagery. Boorstin notes that in the past, "A public man needed a private secretary for a barrier between himself and the public. Nowadays he has a press secretary, to keep him properly in the public eye."[20] The age of the image has created a whole industry that specializes in managing the public perceptions of leaders. Even Boorstin, writing with such prescience in the 1960s, could not have predicted how social networking would ensure that each person in the future would have the tools at his fingertips to manage his own "public brand" through the careful manipulation of imagery. Each of us now functions as our own public relations expert. This revolution seemingly has distorted Shakespeare's description of the way in which people find greatness and influence. Now any of us can engineer our own fame in ways not possible in the past.

PLATFORM VS. SPIRITUAL GROWTH

According to an increasing number of marketing experts, leadership today is all about "building platform." It is expected that by working hard at sculpting your public profile that you can have "reach," influencing huge swathes of people. When I studied advertising at college, we were told by our lecturers, all ex-ad men, that the key was to rise above the "clutter," to create advertisements that stood out in a loud and crowded marketplace. This advice was given to us as students who would soon be working for companies, yet now such advice is given to all individuals. We are told that the world is more competitive, more crowded than ever before. Therefore we must create a platform to stand out above the crowd and make our voice heard in order to get our message or product into the hands of the right people. I totally understand this idea; I write as someone who has crafted advertisements. I write as someone who writes books that I believe in. Yet I also realize that there is a danger in all of this. There is a line that can be unwittingly crossed today when it comes to understanding what it is to lead. We can start to forget where our message begins and where we end. We can forget that we are communicating the gospel and end up broadcasting ourselves.

Like sexuality or money, being "known" by a large group of people is not a sin in itself; it is made holy or unholy by virtue of whether or not it points toward God. I myself use Twitter, I have written a blog, and I have witnessed how such technologies can contribute to ministry. Yet I also understand the danger that they can present to one's soul especially as it has the potential to rouse the deep monster within.

You see, at school I struggled tremendously. My unrecognized battles with my mental health made school quite difficult. I often had terrible grades. I began to believe that I was hopeless, that I was unable to complete tasks that others found easy. I believed that I was stupid. I remember one time in high school I was sitting in class working on an assignment on Shakespeare's *Macbeth*. While the other students seemed to move easily through the assignment, my mind became a web of knots, my palms began to sweat. My lack of self-confidence in my ability overtook me.

The bell for the end of class sounded and all of the other students were allowed to go home. My teacher asked me to stay until I finished the assignment. As I sat there, for the first time a sense of confidence overtook me. The play seemed to open up, I sensed themes and narrative arcs, I understood the characters and what Shakespeare was trying to achieve. My self-doubt disappeared and a stream of words flowed from my pen. Overjoyed that I had finished what I thought was a genuinely good piece of work, my teacher then accused me of cheating, reading through the textbook to find the passages that she believed I had copied. I was utterly devastated. A sense of injustice burned in me. The freedom and confidence that I had felt whilst writing was destroyed. This sense of hopelessness would follow me to college and to seminary.

This persistent sense of hopelessness reared its head one day on Twitter. I had tweeted my observations of a recent event in the news and had forgotten about it. My friend emailed me telling me that a leading overseas newspaper had reprinted my tweet, commenting that my text was the most intelligent response to the incident in question. Automatically, my cursor went to the tweet button, so that I could let my Twitter followers know what this newspaper had said about me. The next second I came to my senses. I asked myself, Why on earth do my followers need to know what this newspaper said about me? What good does this do the promotion of the gospel? Does this encourage others? Does this get my books into the hands of people who will be grown in Christ by them?

The only reason why I would push the tweet button is because deep down I feared that I was hopeless, that I was not smart enough, not good enough—that somehow this newspaper making this comment proved my intelligence. I was about to boast because of an unresolved issue that I had not truly brought before God. I was not communicating the values of the kingdom—in fact, I was contradicting them. I refrained. As I looked at my Twitter feed later that day, I saw multiple well-known Christian leaders retweeting compliments that others had given them. There is nothing wrong with receiving compliments from others; encouragements are fantastic things that can keep us going in our leadership.

YET WHEN IT BECOMES THE NORM TO LET EVERYONE KNOW THE NICE THINGS PEOPLE ARE SAYING ABOUT US VERSUS THE MESSAGES WE CREATE FOR

THE KINGDOM, THEN WE HAVE A CULTURAL PROBLEM.

Our time and culture of platform and self-promotion forces us to ask some hard questions. Would we be willing to believe that God chooses how far and wide our influence goes? Are we happy to allow God to be our PR agent even if it means a life of unrecognized service?

AS LEADERS, INFLUENCERS, AND CREATIVES, WE ALL HAVE DREAMS. WOULD WE BE SATISFIED IF GOD MADE THOSE DREAMS COME TRUE BUT WE RECEIVED NO PERSONAL RECOGNITION?

HOLLOW AT THE CORE

Stanley understood that the emerging world of media and technology offered him a chance at reinvention. It would be easy for us to write Stanley off as a violent self-promoter. Indeed he was. Yet reading his accounts of his journey, no matter how sculptured and self-serving they are, he genuinely believed he was doing good. He was truly passionate about the eradication of slavery, and he saw himself as an evangelistic light bringing the gospel to Africa. However the new media landscape that turned Henry Morton Stanley from anonymity to global celebrity was unable to shape his inner being. On the ground, his personal storms overtook him. Having crafted his own fame, his inner core was empty.

The great twentieth-century poet T. S. Eliot was obsessed with Conrad's *Heart of Darkness*. For him this tale of empty men, driven mad by greed and violence as they tried to make their mark on the world, reflected a dark turn in Western culture. His poem "The Hollow Men" was inspired in large part by Conrad's tale.

> We are the hollow men
> We are the stuffed men
> Leaning together
> Headpiece stuffed with straw. Alas
> Our dried voices, when
> We whisper together
> Are quiet and meaningless.[21]

Our culture needs to hear clear voices proclaiming a different way. Yet because of our hollowness, our words are reduced to mere whispers, "quiet and meaningless." We may be able to make ourselves appear like heroes coming down from the sky, surrounded by clouds of self-constructed importance. However, this will not help us slay Leviathan; self-focused celebrity status does not create effective, Christ-centered leaders. Those who lead must attempt to remedy the chaos that has overtaken the world, yet if we are not careful, the chaos of the very culture we are trying to save can exacerbate that void, that depravity. The cautionary lesson from the life of Henry Morton Stanley and the moral of *Heart of Darkness* is that the hollow heroes can very easily let their own dark madness burst forth, becoming chaos monsters themselves.

WITHOUT REALIZING IT, LEADERS CAN PAINT THEIR OWN DYSFUNCTION OVER CHURCHES, MINISTRIES, AND MISSION FIELDS. ALL TOO EASILY, THE EFFORT TO PREACH THE GOSPEL BECOMES ABOUT APPEASING FEARS AND INSECURITIES, TURNING

LEADERSHIP INTO A TOOL USED TO PRIMARILY GAIN A SENSE OF PERSONAL MEANING.

We can exploit the places and people that God has called us to in order to gain a sense of identity. Historian A. N. Wilson suggests, "Stanley saw Africa, as many explorers and missionaries did, as the metaphor for the uncharted territory of their own personal 'struggle.'"[22] We must examine the ways in which we have attempted to turn our own ministries, workplaces, and mission fields into the playgrounds of our own personal struggles. We must search our hearts for the ways in which our own insecurities and wounded egos sabotage the gospel message that we have been entrusted with. We must become leaders who are deep in a society of the spectacle that produces shallowness.

PART VI

THE BAPTIZED LEADER

Adventure becomes an act of revolt, an access to the underworld of romantic energies.

—PAUL ZWEIG, *The Adventurer*

THE IDOL OF CHRISTIAN ADVENTURE

A number of years ago, I planned an extremely creative worship service. The Christians who were there loved it. They thought that it was fantastic because it was so unconventional, so "unlike church." After the service I received effusive praise. People told me that this was exactly the kind of innovative approach that the church in the twenty-first century needed in order to remain relevant. Just when my head was about to explode with overinflation, I overheard a non-Christian visitor sharing his frustrations with the service. He had reached a spiritual crossroads and was looking for some good news that there was something bigger. He wanted to pray, to hear from the Bible, to find out whether there really was a God. He hated my creative service; it only left him confused. I realized that the Christians who loved the service were more motivated by our insecurity than we were by genuinely listening to the voices of unchurched people.

Emptiness seeks out thrills and excitement to escape the mundane. When this happens in Christian circles, churches recast mission, ministry, and leadership as adventures. Theologian Rod Thompson tells the story of visiting a church that was sending a group of its young people off on a mission trip to work with former child soldiers in Uganda.[1] Thompson was shocked to see that the two-week trip was "sold" to the congregation as an adventure. Yet one would have to wonder, would the child soldiers living in abject poverty and having suffered war trauma see their lives as exciting and adventurous?

The concept of adventure is deeply connected to the Babylonian, pagan idea of the hero. The human who, through travel, experiences acts of glory can traverse the divide between the humans and gods. The author Paul Zweig saw the recapturing of adventure as an essential means of finding meaning in the modern world and escaping what he saw as the confining nature of relationships, routine, and normality. While this sounded good in theory, the practice of finding adventure in the modern world was more difficult for Zweig, who would set off for the Sahara Desert. Instead of finding adventure, he found sandstorms. Zweig was hit with the reality that he could not escape himself. The old maxim "Wherever you go there you are" was palpably true. Despite discovering this new creed of adventure as a medicine to the modern disease of meaninglessness, Zweig would still feel "The experience of inner emptiness, the frightening feeling that at some level of existence I'm nobody, that my identity has collapsed and deep down no one's there."[2]

Zweig contracted cancer in his forties, with the illness eventually taking his life. He would discover that adventure loses most of its draw to someone dying of a terminal illness. The relationships that he had run away from now meant everything.

DYING TO SELF

CHRISTIAN LEADERSHIP IS A STRANGE BEAST. IN

ITS TRUEST FORM IT RUNS COUNTER TO ALMOST EVERYTHING THE WORLD HAS TAUGHT US: TO CREATE OURSELVES BY ACCUMULATING RICHES, EXPERIENCES, AND RELATIONSHIPS, AND, MOST IMPORTANTLY, TO BROADCAST THEM TO THE AUDIENCE THAT WILL MIRROR BACK TO US THE MESSAGES WE WISH TO HEAR.

The gospel asks us to do the opposite of this. Out of Jesus' mouth is uttered the strange, jarring commandment: "Whoever wants to be my disciple must deny themselves and take up their cross daily and follow me" (Luke 9:23).

Jesus asks us to not just die, but to take up a daily discipline of dying, to look not to an audience for a sense of self, but to follow Him. Perhaps, especially in our culture, such a commandment feels like jumping into the dark unknown. The kind of life that Jesus proposes is not an escape from the everyday or Zweig's attempt to break from ourselves. Such a life asks that we truly encounter ourselves, to come face-to-face with our brokenness, sin, fears, and insecurities. It challenges us to repudiate the pagan belief that we can cross the border between humanity and divinity. The gospel teaches us that this border is impassable and the only way to discover life is to deny oneself and follow Christ.

Returning to Jonah, for him and the crew of the stricken vessel caught in the divine storm, the myth of the hero was destroyed. Heroes can battle armies, they can defeat giants. They can climb mountains and cross raging rivers. Yet no human can defeat a storm. A storm shifts. It is fluid, unpredictable. The strongest champions and the greatest armies of the world cannot defeat the wind. As the ship breaks up, the crew have tossed the cargo overboard. They have been unable to coax and cajole their gods into coming to their rescue. Before salvation and rescue can come, Jonah must admit that there is nothing he can do. At its heart, biblical faith is a creed of the antihero. It is the story of men and women who come to the end of themselves and must discover God. The biblical antihero is the direct counterpoint to the pagan hero. Jonah now understands this. He tells the crew, "Pick me up and throw me into the sea, and it will become calm" (Jonah 1:12).

With one last attempt to reach for the heroic, the crew try to row back to land. But they cannot beat the power of the divine storm. It is time for a different approach. The Hebrew in the hold called to live a different vision of life knows intuitively what it is to act in ways that rub against the grain. His only option is to enact what should be a routine, non-adventurous response: surrender and repentance. "I know that it is my fault that this great storm has come upon you" (Jonah 1:12).

Jonah is now acting according to his call. He is acting as a leader. Commanding the crew to throw him into the sea is a prophetic act. Yet this prophetic act can only be expressed through repentance. The crew now follows his command. Jonah has a willing audience but he has nothing to gain. After awakening from his slumber— the first step of leadership—the second step of leadership is one of confession. This is not platform, this is public repentance. The Hebrew in the hold, through his simple words and powerful command, paints a tapestry of confession, contrition, and repentance. Jonah is not just being thrown into the sea, he is being baptized, dying to self as a public proclamation of his trust in God.

For Jonah this is not a symbolic act, it is very real. Jonah is surrounded by sea, a watery embodiment of fear, and a profound metaphor for disconnection from relationships and God. In the sea there is no audience, only death. The churning sea recalls the world before creation, before light, life, and land. When "The earth was formless and empty, darkness was over the surface of the deep" (Genesis 1:2).

To be thrown into the sea undoes creation. Jonah is returned to what the Hebrews called *Sheol,* the place of the dead. Jonah must fear that the consequences of being thrown into the sea will result in him being unmade, wiped out of existence. Yet strangely, in the upside-down world of the biblical imagination, in such a dark situation there is light. When hopelessness seems the order of the day, hope can still be found. When Genesis describes the unmade world as formless and empty, while darkness covers the world, we are told that, "The Spirit of God was hovering over the waters" (Genesis 1:2).

In the language of the Bible, God's Spirit is linked to both water and wind. To be thrown into the sea seemingly cuts us off from God and from life. Yet in God's reality it is to be subsumed in His

Spirit. This is a hard lesson. It contradicts almost everything we understand about the mechanics of life. How can being thrown into your ultimate fears and cast into the abyss of death lead to life? Yet it does. Jonah, now living out his call as a prophetic leader illustrates this counterintuitive truth with the example of his own life: the truth that God is found in death.

THIS IS THE SIGN OF JONAH OF WHICH CHRIST WOULD LATER SPEAK. IT IS A RESURRECTION TRUTH THAT GETS OBSCURED IN A WORLD OF DARKNESS, AND IT MUST BE ILLUMINATED BY PROPHETIC ACTIONS OF LEADERS, INFLUENCERS, AND CREATIVES WHO HAVE DIED TO SELF.

LEADERSHIP IS THE ACT OF DYING TO SELF IN PUBLIC

Through the leadership actions of Jonah, the ship to Tarshish is transformed. This is no longer a carrier of luxury goods; the cargo was thrown overboard at the onset of the storm. This is no longer a pagan vessel; the idols of the crew have been exhausted. This is no longer the passage to another life; the allure of adventure had been blown away by the vicious winds. A mysterious change is occurring upon the boat and the symbols and signs are shifting. This ship of Tarshish, a symbol of wealth, consumer goods, and the power and potential of a better life is now being made holy. It is being sanctified.

Jonah now has an audience. They are desperately looking to him to lead. If he was to perform a heroic act, his audience would remain precisely that, an audience. They would remain mired in passivity, looking to him for salvation. Yet through his act of surrender, through his public death to self, there is a very different reaction, and the audience become worshipers: "At this the men greatly feared the Lord, and they offered a sacrifice to the Lord and made vows to him" (Jonah 1:16). Jonah's act of leadership has turned the crew into a community marked by sacrifice, worship, and gratitude to God. God's grace in calming the sea now fills the vessel. God has been vindicated.

When leaders die to pushing their own agendas and realize that leadership is the act of dying to self, those around them are profoundly transformed. Selfless leadership opens a space for God to flow into. All Jonah could do was to repent and surrender. He could not even heroically throw himself overboard. All he could do was to give up the illusion of control and autonomy in the face of God's storm and surrender himself to the crew who would do the throwing.

WITHDRAWAL-RETURN

In his sweeping meditation of human history, Arnold J. Toynbee noted that cultures are healed and rejuvenated by creative minorities led by creative leaders. Toynbee noted that before this healing work could begin, the creative leader must engage in what he labeled "withdrawal-return."[3] To break the spell that society has over them, the creative leader must withdraw from her society. Once the leader has withdrawn away from the influence of the society, he or she can no longer look to it for a sense of identity and meaning. Meaning must be found elsewhere—outside of the society.

IT IS THROUGH THE PROCESS OF WITHDRAWAL THAT THE LEADER DISCOVERS THE MYTHS AND ILLUSIONS OF THE CULTURE FROM WHICH HE IS APART. THE LEADER GAINS CRITICAL DISTANCE.

Our culture understands this principle, but only in part. We understand that "getting away" can be refreshing, that absence makes the heart grow fonder, but the kind of withdrawal that we encounter in the story of Jonah and other influential leaders is radically different.

When we withdraw of our own accord, seeking adventure and the exotic, we may gain distance from our society, yet we are still in control. We need to understand the way in which our culture's myths and illusions have penetrated the depths of our inner self. We can only gain this insight when we are forced to totally surrender and die to self. When we are withdrawn from our society — which shapes and forms our beliefs, actions, and habits—we are only left with our inner world. With the noise and distraction of our society now gone, God's Word is the dominant sound. It can begin its healing work in us.

In our world of platform and social networking, we all too easily fall into the danger of being more concerned with our audience than our inner world. Our inner world remains unhealed and undeveloped because we never truly experience withdrawal. There is no room for reflection or privacy. Instead we prepare each thought, action, and experience for broadcast. With the proliferation of the Internet, we can be sitting on the other side of the planet yet still connected to our culture, still dependent on it to give us a sense of self. Often then God will not use physical withdrawal to remove us from our culture. Withdrawal and periods of wilderness may come from illness, relational conflict, or unemployment. It can also come from social distance that leadership creates. Many who seek after leadership in order to "be known" and then in turn loved are dismayed when they discover how loneliness and isolation follow the office of leadership. Yet God uses this isolation to create a dependency upon Him.

THE CIRCLE OF FRIENDS

For many younger leaders one of the great challenges of withdrawal is moving outside of what Adam Curtis calls the "circle of friends."[4] Curtis believes that the circle of friends is one of the great ideologies of our day. He notes that increasingly, TV shows and movies are centered around small groups of friends, not individuals. Reality shows feature similar groupings, and this trend is starting to influence how news is presented. Curtis believes that as the world becomes more complicated and our trust in institutions erodes, our small group of friends becomes the primary source of authority in our lives. Those who shape media understand that no longer do we look to a singular authority figure; instead we are more easily convinced when information is presented by a grouping of virtual peers. On TV shows like *The View,* the audience members, watching far away at home, feel like they are sitting in on an intimate discussion of friends, when in reality they are being sold an ideology. We are far more susceptible to being influenced because inherently as humans we fear going against the group. We are suckers for peer group pressure. A singular voice seems like an opinion, a group agreeing feels like consensus.

We replicate these groupings in our personal lives. If you examine the circle of friends closely, there is an inherent narcissism at play as people seek out friends who mirror their own opinions and views of the world. These small groupings become a way of dealing with the *anomie* that modern culture brings, in many cases allowing the individual to have their narrow view of the world reinforced. In our culture of hedonism, the circle of friends seemingly allows us a modicum of relational solace but also maximum personal freedom. In sitcoms such as *Friends* or *How I Met Your Mother*, sexual partners can be swapped, but the integrity of the circle of friends must remain intact. In the democratic, egalitarian spirit of our day, we hold in suspicion positions of social authority, yet we submit to the power of peers. Social anxiety, peer group pressure, and competition all dictate our lives. Many are more afraid of offending their friends than they are of offending figures of authority. We have moved from a culture based upon hierarchy to a peerarchy. Ironically we flee from relational distinctions and boundaries, yet without these traditions and boundaries we become mired in codependency.

I have discovered that one of the great fears of younger leaders is stepping out of the circle of friends. Many ask whether it's possible to lead your peers, but the real question is: Does one have to sacrifice the circle of friends in order to lead? The totality of Jonah's immersion into the deep tells us yes.

THE LEADER MUST STEP OUT FROM THE TYRANNY OF THE CIRCLE OF FRIENDS.

The biblical leader understands the importance of relationships, but also understands that God chooses and appoints some to lead. Therefore the biblical leader understands that a distinction must be made. Yes, we can have friends, but there are times when for the sake of the gospel and the kingdom we must withdraw from our social relationships. The biblical leader cannot submit to authorities who are not God, even when those authorities are our friends.

SMASHING THE MIRROR

Toynbee noted that Jesus' life, death, and resurrection was the example of withdrawal-return par excellence. In fact the whole sweep of Scripture reflects this reality. Moses must withdraw to the mountain. The people of God must wander in the desert. Ezekiel must be sent into exile in Babylon. David must suffer a coup at the hands of his son and be thrown out of his capital. Jesus at the beginning of His ministry withdraws to the wilderness. He would continue to do so throughout His ministry, retreating to meet with His Father. Speaking to leaders, Henri Nouwen notes that it was in His time in the desert that Jesus was tempted by Satan toward a kind of heroic, spectacular ministry, a mode of ministry that would win Him both applause and an audience. "But Jesus refused to be a stunt man. He did not come to walk on hot coals, swallow fire, or put his hand in the lion's mouth to demonstrate that he had something worthwhile to say."[5]

For Nouwen, his personal withdrawal would occur at the height of his popularity as an author and speaker as he left a prestigious academic position to work with disabled people at a Christian community. His peers were concerned with this strange move. Yet among his disabled friends, Nouwen would learn powerful spiritual lessons in what it is to depend upon God. No longer could Nouwen leave the office and do what he wanted to do; he was immersed in a community of people who depended upon him for who he was, not what he did. His disabled friends did not care that he was a renowned author and speaker, they simply accepted him based on his kind personality. Nouwen's care for one profoundly disabled man named Adam would in Nouwen's final years teach him profound spiritual lessons. These lessons were captured in his powerful book *Adam*. This man who lived in absolute obscurity, who needed constant care, taught Nouwen what it is to truly depend upon God.

Such miracles, grounded in the dust of the ordinary, can only happen when one allows themselves to be thrown into the abyss.

IRONICALLY, WHEN THE LEADER DISCOVERS THAT THEY CAN DO NOTHING IN THEIR OWN POWER, A NEW KIND OF POWER EMANATES FROM THEIR LIFE: THEY GAIN SPIRITUAL AUTHORITY.

This is the way of Jesus' upside-down kingdom. Jesus would preach,

> I am the true vine, and my Father is the gardener. He cuts off every branch in me that bears no fruit, while every branch that does bear fruit he prunes so that it will be even more fruitful. You are already clean because of the word I have spoken to you. Remain in me, as I also remain in you. No branch can bear fruit by itself; it must remain in the vine. Neither can you bear fruit unless you remain in me. (John 15:1–4)

WHEN WE WITHDRAW, WE LEARN NEW MOVEMENTS. WE MOVE FROM STRIVING TO ABIDING, FROM COMPETING TO COMMUNING, FROM BROADCASTING TO BEING. WE MAKE A BREAK WITH THE ANXIETY THAT DRIVES SO MUCH OF MODERN LIFE AND, SADLY, SO MUCH OF CONTEMPORARY LEADERSHIP.

NON-ANXIOUS LEADERSHIP

At the funeral of former British Prime Minister Margaret Thatcher, the media became transfixed by the sight of a young woman giving a Bible reading. Amanda Thatcher, the nineteen-year-old granddaughter of Margaret Thatcher and a committed Christian, captured the world's attention by reading Paul's teaching on spiritual warfare in chapter six of the book of Ephesians. What shocked the media and the attending public figures was that a nineteen-year-old could speak with such poise, calmness, and authority without breaking down into a blubbering mess at the funeral of a loved one. There is absolutely nothing wrong with being emotional at a funeral. No one would have condemned Amanda Thatcher for breaking down. She stood out because such a calm, authoritative, and secure display by a young person is so rare in the contemporary climate. Amanda Thatcher had a non-anxious presence.

Anxiety is one of the strange constants of the modern, comfortable West. At the end of the nineteenth century, as the society of the spectacle was birthed, a new kind of social illness was born. The neurologist George Miller Beard around 1869 coined the term *neurasthenia* to describe a new kind of stress-driven illness that was sweeping through modern urban environments. The press labeled the phenomenon *American nervousness*. Sufferers experienced exhaustion, depression, suicidal thoughts, and anxiety. Beard believed that the highly stimulating, competitive, and stressful contemporary culture was causing the illness. In Vienna, a quickly modernizing Sigmund Freud set out to cure well-to-do women from the effects of hysteria, a condition that was believed to cause emotional imbalance, fear, and anxiety. In our day, anxiety has reached epidemic proportions in the West. Worry, fear, and stress define the contemporary emotional landscape. Rabbi and psychologist Edwin H. Friedman in his study of leadership argues that contrary to popular opinion, leadership is not in the possession of particular skills, traits, or personal attributes. It is primarily in the ability to command a non-anxious persona in an anxious environment.[6]

Friedman lived and worked in Washington, DC, studying how leadership worked in Jewish and Christian congregations, government departments, the military, corporate entities, as well as marriages and families. He found that all of these environments contained high levels of anxiety that would inevitably turn toxic. People seek out others who are experiencing the same levels of anxiety in order to feel a sense of support. However according to Friedman, this only made things worse, as the anxiety spread like a contagion. Friedman came to believe that Western culture as a whole had been overtaken by fear and anxiety, which ultimately made the task of leadership highly difficult.

In such an environment, leaders are increasingly afraid of offending others. In a world shaped by the circle of friends, many people fear being autocratic, directive leaders and prefer instead the relational matrix of the organic values. The goal is to keep consensus and relational harmony when in reality these people become fearful, passive carriers of anxiety. An obsession with consensus becomes paralyzing as toxic factors in the working environment are allowed to continue.

When somebody embodies a non-anxious presence in a toxic environment two things happen. Firstly, people become drawn to the person who embodies a non-anxious presence, just as the world's attention was drawn to Amanda Thatcher. Secondly, anxious people work to sabotage the leader, because they are a threat to the environment in which anxiety is the norm.

TO SURVIVE AND EFFECT
POSITIVE CHANGE THE LEADER
MUST LEARN TO SEPARATE
FROM THE TOXIC ENVIRONMENT
AND ULTIMATELY LEARN HOW
TO EMOTIONALLY WITHDRAW
AND RETURN. BY GAINING
EMOTIONAL DISTANCE
THE LEADER CAN RETURN,
EMBODYING A POSTURE OF
PEACE, WHICH ALTHOUGH
INITIALLY RESISTED WILL

EVENTUALLY HEAL THE

ENVIRONMENT.

To summarize:

- Leadership is not so much about skill and technique as it is about allowing God to transform your inner world of anxieties, fears, and insecurities.

- The leader will exist in a toxically anxious environment that both desires leadership and works to undermine it.

- In order to influence with authority, the leader must go through a process of withdrawal. Here the leader learns to confront their own anxiety, and emotionally differentiate themselves from others and the anxious environments that they create.

- The leader must "return" to the toxic environment, maintaining relational connection yet remaining emotionally differentiated, and live out a posture of peace.

LEADING FROM YOUR PAIN

As I made peace with what God was allowing in my life, my concern became the question, How do I lead during this challenge? Getting to church required the logistical planning of the Allied landing at Normandy.

We would arrive as church was starting and leave right when church ended. The relational connections that I could normally generate with new people began to disappear. I believed strongly in relational leadership, and began to feel like a fraud as a leader.

However, I realized that God was doing something different. I was being taught that my

LEADERSHIP POWER COMES NOT FROM WHAT I AM DOING BUT WHAT HE IS DOING INSIDE OF ME.

I could not travel. My sermon preparation was clouded by constant exhaustion. The spaces and times in which God seemed to speak to me had disappeared in the melee of sterilized bottles, night feedings, food preparation, and an endless changing of diapers.

I could only do the essentials. I would arrive at my desk in the morning, exhausted by the night before, my mind racing with thoughts, panic attacks washing over me. I remember reading one of the brochures that the hospital gives you when you are going to have twins. It had a section written by a father of twins, who during the first year of his twins' lives would come home from work and often stand at his front door for five minutes, unable to enter into the chaos inside after a busy day at the office. I would come home for work, desperate for reprieve. My wife, family, and friends were fantastic help. Yet when you are experiencing a mixed episode, every sound is heightened. When chaos and stimulation are like a form of torture, coming home to a house of screaming twins, to another night of endless chores and sleeplessness, seemed utterly impossible. Yet I would do it. The sun would come up, the world would not end. You keep going.

I had finally engaged a wonderful mentor named Terry. In our first message over Skype, as I shared with him what I had been going through, I still remember him waving at the screen, telling me, "Mark, you have to stop, you are in severe burnout. You have to take a break immediately." I acknowledged the wisdom of Terry's advice. However, there was a problem. That winter everyone around me was leaving for sunnier climates. My coworker Sarah, who is the heart and soul of keeping the church running, had been donated a summer sabbatical at an overseas seminary. Other staff were taking long vacations. Board members, confidants I trust in the church, all were deserting the city. There was no way that I could take a break at such short notice. These absences did not just mean that I would be holding the fort alone. It meant that I would have to carry parts of other people's roles. I was already exhausted and I would have to increase my already busy schedule. On top of this, our church had recently purchased a property and was just starting a redevelopment. The temptation to compare your lot with others kicked in. I have never known so many of my other peers in ministry to take sabbaticals at one time. It felt like I was surrounded by people who were taking the break that I deserved.

My mental health continued to plague me. Bipolarity can be affected by the seasons, and winter was never a good time for me. So I did something that I promised I would never do. I made an ultimatum with God. I told Him that He must miraculously deliver me a break. I waited, knowing that my request was ridiculous, but I was angry at God. As frustrated as I was, I kept waiting for a sign. My wife and I finally had a chat that I thought we would never have. We sat until three in the morning discussing whether I should quit ministry. The whole next day I felt sick with worry. I was at the end of myself. Then the sign came.

It was the early evening of Monday, my scheduled day off. God told me very clearly to get in my car and go to the last place I wanted to be, our church. I went into the old house situated on our church property, sat on the old carpet, turned on the heater, and fumed. God again clearly spoke to me. I was to come here every Monday night on my day off and wait on Him. He told me that for the next seven weeks I was to study Psalm 18. I picked up the Bible and began to read. I was hoping for encouragement. Instead I was confronted with the following,

In my distress I called to the Lord;
  I cried to my God for help.
From his temple he heard my voice;
  my cry came before him, into his ears.
The earth trembled and quaked,
  and the foundations of the mountains shook;
  they trembled because he was angry.
Smoke rose from his nostrils;
  consuming fire came from his mouth,
  burning coals blazed out of it.
He parted the heavens and came down;
  dark clouds were under his feet.
He mounted the cherubim and flew;
  he soared on the wings of the wind.
He made darkness his covering, his canopy around him—
  the dark rain clouds of the sky.
Out of the brightness of his presence clouds advanced,
  with hailstones and bolts of lightning.
The Lord thundered from heaven;
  the voice of the Most High resounded.
He shot his arrows and scattered the enemy,
  with great bolts of lightning he routed them.
The valleys of the sea were exposed
  and the foundations of the earth laid bare

at your rebuke, Lord,
at the blast of breath from your nostrils. (Psalm 18:6–15)

I did not want the God who would come in a storm, with fire, smoke, and lightning. I did not want the God who rebukes with blasts of breath from His nostrils. I wanted the God who would give me a nice big hug and then offer me free plane tickets to a sunny retreat away from the storm. God then spoke clearly a third time. He told me to walk to the kitchenette and open the cupboard. I did so. At the back of the cupboard was a very small bowl. For the fourth time that night I clearly heard Him speak. *Mark, for the next six weeks, I want you to only eat a meal each day that you can fit in this small bowl.* I picked up the bowl in my hand. It would struggle to fit half an orange. I raised the bowl above my head ready to smash it across the kitchen floor. God then spoke for the last time that night. He told me, *This is your break.*

I was incensed. I asked for a break, a respite from ministry, some solace from the battle with mental health, from the exhaustion. My "break" would not consist of a sabbatical filling my spiritual and emotional tanks, nor a vacation, resting my body and mind. Instead my "break" would involve me coming into the office on my day off to study a Psalm about God coming in a storm while I fasted my already exhausted body.

I obeyed. Despite my anger, He was right.

Our contemporary culture, even our Christian leadership culture, has taught us that when we see a storm coming, we should run the other way, we should retreat, take a break. God would teach me over those seven weeks to walk into the storm, to encounter the God who loves to meet His people in the storm. God was asking me to withdraw, not away to the comfort of a sabbatical, but into the swirling, blasting winds of His storm.

LEADERS DO NOT AVOID THE STORM WHEN IT COMES, INSTEAD THEY STEP INTO THE MAELSTROM AND DISCOVER HE WHO COMES IN THE STORM.

THE LORD IS NEAR

Withdrawal-return is an easy motif to remember yet it is extraordinarily difficult to enact. To be a non-anxious presence of peace in the storm that is our stress-filled, competitive society of the spectacle is a life's work, one that can only be achieved by emotionally withdrawing from the habit of looking to our culture, to its mirrors, to its measurements of worth. As Paul reminds us in his letter to the church in Philippi, "Do not be anxious about anything, but in every situation, by prayer and petition, with thanksgiving, present your requests to God. And the peace of God, which transcends all understanding, will guard your hearts and your minds in Christ Jesus" (Philippians 4:6–7).

This verse is often quoted, yet the short, powerful sentence that precedes it is often left out: "The Lord is near." All of the peace that follows can only come when we live out of the reality that He is near. For Jonah, the sea was the abyss, a place seemingly absent of God. In this abyss lived chaos monsters that warred with God. Yet

Jonah would discover that in the belly of the beast at the bottom of the sea, God was near. To lead and to speak God's Word that ushered in a new creation in the city of Nineveh, he must withdraw and understand that God is near.

PART VII

THE OPPOSITIONAL POSTURE

Another option was to romanticize rebellion and resistance for its own sake. Resistance to mainstream society was often seen as therapeutic for the individual, and promoted on those grounds.

—JOSEPH HEATH AND ANDREW POTTER, *Nation of Rebels*

THE ORGANIC VALUES: A NEW SOCIAL POSTURE

Édouard Manet's painting *Le déjeuner sur l'herbe* shocked and tantalized audiences when it was exhibited in 1863 at the *Salon des Refusés*, the exhibition for those artists deemed too modern for the more classically inclined salon. Manet's painting was shocking because it contained a woman, naked, sitting in a park with two young men. There was nothing particularly shocking about a naked woman in a painting at the time. The neoclassicists favored by the establishment painted plenty of naked women. Yet these naked bodies were always placed in classical environments, illustrating characters from the Greek myths. What was alarming to the general public with Manet's painting was the context of its contained nudity. It featured a naked woman, sitting next to two fully dressed males, who appeared to be having a luncheon in a Parisian park. It was a totally contemporary image.

Paris knew that prostitution existed in some parks around the city. It also knew that a new sexual code was emerging. *Le déjeuner sur l'herbe* not only exposed this underbelly of the city, it seemed to flaunt it, celebrate it. It was not just the exposed flesh that made the picture controversial, it was also the dress of the young men who wore the latest urban fashions. Why weren't the men working? What was this sordid picnic? What was this dangerous yet enticing world where sex and leisure seemed to exist without shame and guilt? The picture superficially seemed to reject the political yet it was a deeply political piece of propaganda. It was a symbol of what the philosopher and historian Lewis Mumford would later call the "utopia of the picnic": a dream of a world of pleasure, devoid of responsibility and work. It represented a new kind of revolution, sparked by a new kind of revolutionary. This was not a revolution that aimed to topple unjust social inequality or upturn the economic landscape, rather it was a moral revolution disguised as an artistic and creative uprising.

THE BOHEMIAN

The poet Charles Baudelaire rebelled against the mechanical values and became one of the most famous men living in Paris at the end of the nineteenth century. Repulsed by the politeness and conventions of the emerging middle-class mainstream, Baudelaire instead dreamed of a new way of interacting with Paris, facilitating a hub for creativity and radical artistic endeavor, one that would shock and provoke the middle classes. Baudelaire communicated this vision throughout his life, but the crystallizing of his approach would be contained in his essay "The Painter of Modern Life." This essay would not only name and shape an emerging group in Paris, but its influence can be felt strongly in our day, shaping the worldview of the creative classes of the West. Baudelaire desired to fund a cultural renaissance in this new urban environment, a cross-pollination of painters, writers, poets, and bohemian vagabonds.

The old order of citizens, and the even older order of the aristocracy, had been joined by a new class of upwardly mobile middle-class consumers. In contrast, Baudelaire proposed a new kind of consumer. His version would not purchase material products but would rather consume the sights, sounds, and experiences of the city in a quest for beauty and art. This man to Baudelaire was a new kind of artist, one whose art was their life. "Not a single one of his drawings is signed . . . Yet all of his works are signed—with his dazzling soul . . . He is rapturously breathing in all the odours and essences of life . . . He marvels at the eternal beauty and the amazing harmony of life in the capital cities."[1] Baudelaire was naming an entire subculture of young, arty men who lived in late-nineteenth-century Paris. These young men adopted the stance of cynicism. Baudelaire praised those who could retain a cold distance. Even though Paris was transforming, the memory of violence was still palpable pandemonium of revolution hung over Parisian culture. Thus this new creative identity was a protective suit. The blasé attitude was developed and worn as a shield, protecting the individual from the cultural storms. The threat of constant change meant that the future remained unpredictable, thus the bohemian remained moored to the present moment. They were individualists who seemed to hover around the edges of the fruits of modern culture, frequenting cafes, nightclubs, and chic urban locales, yet always maintaining their social distance.

THE NEW CREATIVES

Before the revolution, the idea of individuality as we understand it did not exist. People were organized corporately into various groups based on birth, employment, and geography. These groups determined everything, from how much tax you paid, where you could go, and who you could marry. However the revolution changed this, creating the modern individual. Without external indicators of identity, bohemianism allowed self-creation, a set of aristocratic flourishes in a rapidly growing egalitarian culture. It provided a post-traditional way of developing an identity for those who wished to remain in flux. For Baudelaire this new urban personality "Appears above all in periods of transition, when democracy is not yet all-powerful, and aristocracy is only just beginning to totter and fall." It was a "New kind of aristocracy . . . the last spark of heroism."[2] For a culture in flux, unsure how to lead, influence, and create, the bohemian offered a new place to stand, a set of organic values from which to break with the mechanical.

SELLING THE BOHEMIAN EXPERIENCE

With art and creativity as the highest good, the whole of life must be transformed into a creative act. Nature had provided this spark for many of Baudelaire's fellow travelers. However his approach was unique because he recast the city, with all of its masses, movement, and visual culture, as a new kind of landscape of inspiration. As religion faded, art would take its place. Music was elevated as religion was downgraded. A French periodical devoted to this new creative worldview would opine, "In our nineteenth century, a century that no longer believes anything, music has become a kind of religion, a last belief to which society is clinging with all its might, exhausted as it is by dogmas and words."[3] The new creative would not look to a community of faith or to the Bible or to nature for divine inspiration. Instead they would look now to the sensate, the immediate, and the experiential milieu of the city as the font of inspiration.

Today when we speak of the bohemians of Paris, many people think of the Moulin Rouge nightclub. The Moulin Rouge's creators, businessmen Joseph Oller and Charles Zidler, understood the public's hunger for entertainment and their growing visual literacy. The nightclubs and cafes began sponsoring writers and poets to perform at their venues, not just to read their work, but to act the part of the bohemian writer, thus offering their venue an air of "artistic chic." The nightclub featured a myriad of stimulations for the senses. The most famous of these is, of course, the cancan, a frenetic dance originally performed by prostitutes, which pushed the limits of public decency. The bohemian venues such as the Moulin Rouge and the Chat Noir may have sold food, drink, and entertainment, but their primary commodity was a bohemian experience.

> One cabaret dubbed itself "Heaven," placing its visitors among clouds, angels, and harps. Its opposite, the Cabaret de l'Enfer, draped itself in the trappings of hell, its waiters dressed in devil costumes. Clients entered its doors through the gaping mouth of a monster, cut into a facade whose misshapen windows were set off by what seemed a kind of solidified primal ooze, within which the nude bodies of sinners were suspended. Another neighbor styled itself the Cabaret des Truands. Here, customers were confronted by costumed bandits and criminals.[4]

These venues were dealers in disposable identities. According to historian Jerrold Siegel, these establishments offered patrons "a realm of liberated fantasy" and an environment that offered "The release of feelings and emotions that were repressed or restricted in everyday life."[5] The bohemian nightclubs and cafes were simply the other side of the coin of the society of the spectacle; both offered visual and experiential environments. Whereas Gustave Eiffel's department store sold items that promised the consumer respectability and up-to-date fashion, the bohemian environment dealt in the language of shock, controversy, and the breaking of taboos. The clubs offered the "utopia of the picnic" and the upturning of convention. While the middle classes frequented the department stores, spending big on the latest fashions, the bohemians would wear vintage clothes. They favored anything that was unusual, foreign, and different from mainstream taste. From Japanese woodcuts to Central Asian dressing gowns, to Persian slippers, for the bohemians, the world was now a repository of styles, aesthetics, and traditions from which to steal and borrow in the quest for reinvention and differentiation.

The creation of this new urban bohemian space would see the growth of an entire new class of cultural creatives. The revolutionary spirit of Paris, the emerging visual culture, and the bohemian subculture drew artists and the avant-garde to Paris. French bureaucrats, happily promoting their capital as a new mecca of culture and creativity, announced that the number of artists living in the city doubled between 1887 and 1914 and that Paris now had more artists per square mile than in any other place on the globe.

JONAH EXITS THE CITY

There was more going on with the bohemians than just an obsession with art and creativity. Ultimately their position was one of opposition. Reflecting upon the bohemian tradition, Albert Camus would note that the bohemian is "by occupation, always in opposition. He can only exist by defiance."[6] The bohemian's entire identity is wrapped in defining themselves against what they deride as the mainstream. Life for the bohemian is parasitical. Their identity depends on setting themselves against something that if destroyed will ultimately destroy the bohemian. Consequently, the bohemians were never truly radical. They simply embodied a new aristocracy based on elitist consumer choices and lifestyle differentiation. According to cultural historians Heath and Potter, ultimately what the countercultural bohemians did was "romanticize rebellion and resistance for its own sake. Resistance to mainstream society was often seen as therapeutic for the individual, and promoted on those grounds. The goal of improving conditions in society at large, or of promoting social justice, receded from view. In this way, the concern for social justice became redirected and absorbed into an increasingly, narcissistic preoccupation with personal spiritual growth and well-being."[7] However, a third position was created, that opposed both the traditional forces in culture as well as the moderns who supported this change.

Strangely we find Jonah taking such a third position against God and the city of Nineveh. Expelled upon the beach, chastened by God and his encounter with the Leviathan-like fish, Jonah sets out for the pagan metropolis with a sureness in his step. "Jonah obeyed the word of the Lord and went to Nineveh. Now Nineveh was a very large city; it took three days to go through it. Jonah began by going a day's journey into the city, proclaiming, "Forty more days and Nineveh will be overthrown" (Jonah 3:1–4).

Jonah is seemingly now prepared for his mission. He is no longer fleeing the Lord. The city is powerful and huge, its people violent and idolatrous. He will no doubt face resistance or condemnation—perhaps even imprisonment, or death. He seemingly has some kind of plan to deal with this challenge, setting out into the city on what no doubt will be the first act of a great drama. Yet something utterly surprising happens. "The Ninevites believed God. A fast was proclaimed, and all of them, from the greatest to the least, put on sackcloth" (Jonah 3:5).

This city, seemingly so in opposition to God, turns to Him. A culture-wide wave of repentance breaks out. "When Jonah's warning reached the king of Nineveh, he rose from his throne, took off his royal robes, covered himself in sackcloth and sat down in the dust" (Jonah 3:6).

In the ancient world, kings were seen as godlike. As we have learnt, they were made great by heroic acts of courage, grandeur, and glory. His kingship is confirmed by the symbols of royalty: his fine clothing and his elaborate throne. These symbols are discarded, he leaves his throne, he removes his royal clothes, he dispatches with signs that convey his kingship, and he dons sackcloth and sits in the dirt. Imagine this scene played out in our day: The president of the United States, the most powerful person on earth, walks out of the White House, tears off his suit, sends his entourage home, and sits in his underwear in a dirty alleyway amongst garbage, sobbing in broken repentance for his nation.

The king then decrees:

> "By the decree of the king and his nobles: Do not let people or animals, herds or flocks, taste anything; do not let them eat or drink. But let people and animals be covered with sackcloth. Let everyone call urgently on God. Let them give up their evil ways and their violence. Who knows? God may yet relent and with compassion turn from his fierce anger so that we will not perish." When God saw what they did and how they turned from their evil ways, he relented and did not bring on them the destruction he had threatened. (Jonah 3:7–10)

Salvation had come, a turning to God of an unprecedented scale. The king's decree to all the creatures of his kingdom, both human and animal, does not just hint at personal salvation, but even more—a countrywide breaking out of God's shalom. Israel, for so long alone, battling against the surrounding nations, would now have an ally in following the Lord. A pagan, violent culture repented and turned to God. Just as the ship to Tarshish had become a sanctified temple, now a pagan nation was being turned into another kind of Israel. If this was a movie, credits would roll here, perhaps accompanied by a moving montage of Jonah being carried on the shoulders of the Ninevites. The Bible, however, is not Hollywood.

"But to Jonah this seemed very wrong, and he became angry. He prayed to the Lord, "Isn't this what I said, Lord, when I was still at home? That is what I tried to forestall by fleeing to Tarshish. I knew that you are a gracious and compassionate God, slow to anger and abounding in love, a God who relents from sending calamity. Now, Lord take away my life, for it is better for me to die than to live" (Jonah 4:1–3).

Jonah is not happy; he is terribly angry. God has unleashed upon Nineveh a flood of grace rather than a flood of judgment. Jonah's anger reveals a disagreement. His idea of justice is in contrast with God's. He claims that he knew that this would happen all along, justifying his attempted escape to Tarshish. The text tells us that his real excuse for boarding the ship to Tarshish was to escape from the presence of God. Jonah is lying because ultimately he is trying to hide something. He feels that he has lost face. His dignity has been wounded. Despite his step into leadership upon the boat, despite surrendering to the chaos of the storm and the sea monster and, ultimately, despite his crying out to God in the belly of the fish in repentance, Jonah was still carrying an agenda within, a set of expectations about how God should act. He had constructed a worldview of justice that was in contrast with God's.

JONAH THE BOHEMIAN

While grace breaks out over Nineveh, Jonah is now positioned against both God and the repenting nation. He exits Nineveh. The man who could allow himself to be thrown off the side of a ship to his probable death only to find life, now wishes to die. Perhaps as a member of the people chosen and called apart by God, yet who sin and who are tempted by the allure of foreign gods, Jonah is shamed by the contrast between his people's response to God and the wholehearted repentance of Nineveh.

It is no longer Nineveh that faces defeat and destruction but rather Jonah's own worldview. He can allow himself to be thrown into the sea, but he cannot face admitting the way in which he views the world is wrong. A new kind of storm now breaks out, the wind that had brought judgment upon the ship of Tarshish, which then Jonah hoped would obliterate Nineveh, now breaks out in Jonah's inner world. His elitism and self-righteousness are its targets.

Jonah no longer flees from God. He no longer seeks out the foreign delights of Tarshish nor the warm comfort of sleep underneath the decks. Like the bohemians, Jonah creates the third space, the place of critique. He is not with God, nor what God is doing in Nineveh. He sits and watches the city, seemingly waiting for its judgment. He has distanced himself, yet also has placed himself as judge; judge of God and of Nineveh. He sits on the margins in the place of critique, unaware of his own elitism. He does not care about the people of Nineveh, nor does he really care about God's grand project of salvation. Rather he is invested in defending his view of how God should run the world.

Albert Camus called those who followed the bohemian posture in Western culture the Sons of Cain.[8] After murdering his brother, "Cain went out from the Lord's presence and lived in the land of Nod east of Eden" (Genesis 4:16). Jonah now exits Nineveh like Cain headed east. By placing himself on the edge of the city, he still wishes to be involved but at a distance that ensures his own autonomy is kept intact. Jonah—the prophet, the leader—now faces a crisis. There was a simplicity and an honesty to his first flight from God. He simply fled away from God toward Tarshish with all of its temptations. There is a tangible quality to the middle-class temptations of riches, gluttony, and lust. There is an obviousness when people pursue such things. People who had indulged in such sins fell at the feet of Jesus, understanding their own addictive brokenness, their need for God. It was the Pharisees, so close to Christ in their program for religious renewal, who found themselves so far from Him in their spirit of self-righteousness. This is why the organic temptation is far more subtle than its mechanical cousin. The mainstream sins boldly, the bohemian wraps all kinds of intellectual, philosophical, artistic, and even religious scaffolding around their sin. So Jonah sits outside the city facing a new temptation, the temptation of knowing better than God.

This temptation presents itself today. We can sit and watch the Twitter feed, critiquing the methods, models, and ministries of others; from the comfort of our couches we can speculate on how it could be done better. We can devise all kinds of theories, read all the right books, engage in online debate, blog our opinions, yet the whole time be disconnected from actually having skin in the game. Even when our heart is for God's kingdom, if we are not careful we can find ourselves critiquing from the sidelines of God's activity within history. There is a world of difference between pundits and prophets.

AN OLDER SOURCE

Ultimately Jonah believes that his view of the world constitutes the definitive statement on how human life should proceed; he puts himself on God's throne. This model of bohemian living was ultimately built upon a different account of how sin, evil, and brokenness had entered the world, one that differed sharply with the biblical account. This alternate account was a powerful idea popularized by the philosopher Jean-Jacques Rousseau. Until Rousseau, society generally accepted the doctrine of Original Sin.

Yet Rousseau would offer an alternate account of the fall, one that was designed to replace the biblical version. Like the Genesis account of the fall, Rousseau's also started with humans innocently living in unspoiled nature. However, instead of placing the blame for the world's ills squarely on the human heart, he believed that the rules, conventions, and restrictions of society make us unhappy, disconnecting us from our true selves.[9] Rousseau believed that society repressed our naturally innocent, childish, and ultimately happy selves. To be happy again, we need to learn how to bring this inherently joyful self to the surface.

Rousseau's understanding of the natural state of humanity aligns

well with Manet's "utopia of the picnic." If humankind could retreat from politics, responsibility, convention, and tradition they
would discover an Edenic paradise filled with all kinds of hedonistic possibilities. The ideology of the utopia of the picnic did not
point to a flawless future made possible through reason, technology,
and human endeavor. Rather, this alternate vision wanted to retreat
back to the garden of Eden, to return to nature, to that innocent
"inner child." "This rejection of original sin meant a move from a
theocratic to an anthropocentric view of life, from God to man,"[10]
reflects historian Tim Blanning. Thus discipleship was replaced by
self-development, the need for salvation was replaced by the need
for self-expression. Consequently, knowledge received from the establishment must be questioned and taboos must be broken. This
philosophical foundation paved the way for Baudelaire's claim that
this new urban posture of bohemianism was a new religion. Heaven
was a picnic with a naked girl in a park, hell was society.

Mumford claims that the utopia of the picnic is a sham. Firstly,
a picnic only is feasible if there is good weather. Secondly, who
prepares the food, and the wine? Someone with responsibility and
a work ethic must delay their gratification of putting in the hours
to prepare such things. The utopia of picnic, where supposedly we
can simply enjoy life minus rules, work, and responsibility, cannot
exist without a degree of rules, work, and responsibility. Mumford
also notes that what makes a picnic enjoyable is that it is a break
from work and responsibility; a never-ending picnic would in fact
eventually turn into a turgidly boring event.[11] Ultimately the dream
of the utopia of the picnic fails us. Mumford writes that the great
sin of Rousseau's vision was to offer "its disciples a sterile dream:
the hope of a perfect life free from opposition, free from convention, free from compulsion, free from internal conflict."[12] Such a
dream was impossible. In a world of storms, brokenness, and sin,
the utopia of the picnic, like bohemianism, could only live like a

leech, sustaining itself on the existence of the modern world. Offering no practical alternative, it can only offer critique. It can only deconstruct.

JONAH AND HIS SHELTER

Jonah, having stormed outside the city, continues to sit in critique over God and Nineveh. In protest he made himself a shelter, sat in its shade, and waited to see what would happen to the city. The shelter made by Jonah was not simply to keep him out of the sun. The Hebrew tells us that it is a sukkah—a religious booth or temporary shelter used by Jews during the festival of Sukkoth, following the commandment in Leviticus 23:34–44:

> Celebrate this as a festival to the Lord for seven days each year. This is to be a lasting ordinance for the generations to come; celebrate it in the seventh month. Live in temporary shelters for seven days: All native-born Israelites are to live in such shelters so your descendants will know that I had the Israelites live in temporary shelters when I brought them out of Egypt. I am the Lord your God.

Jonah's construction of a sukkah shows that this is not just a simple rebellion, this is a religious protest on the part of Jonah. He has not set up an alternate temple but rather a temporary, rustic, and radical religious space. This is a theologically sophisticated protest against what God is doing in Nineveh. It is an appeal to what, from Jonah's perspective, should be God's approach. Jonah is making a strong reference to the forty years that his people had to suffer in the desert before they truly tasted God's blessing in their homeland, in contrast to the seemingly paltry forty days of repentance that the people of Nineveh will go through. Jonah is now offering a kind of leadership, an influence, rooted in a critique. This is a kind of bohemian-tinged religiosity. It can only exist by protest and critique. The role Jonah plays in the story from here on out is parasitical. This is protest minus the prophetic.

LEADING THROUGH A REBEL POSTURE

One of the great temptations of our day for Christian leaders is to create a Christian version of bohemia. To place ourselves not amongst the poor, the marginalized, or those desperate for the gospel message, but to instead remove ourselves to a place of critique, our own savvy, cutting-edge, self-driven religious spaces that rise up in reaction to what we see as the wrongs of mainstream culture. These spaces appear prophetic, yet when God's wind comes, they reveal themselves as self-serving; their real purpose is to protect our wills, our agenda, our identities. Leaders and creatives of faith who influence from such positions cannot create. They can only critique. They may speak of discipleship, but ultimately they only bring disillusionment.

A whole industry of such deconstructive leadership has sprung up in the West in our day. It is a multimillion-dollar industry that drives book sales, conferences, and consultancy. By all appearances it is focused upon bridging the gap between Christian culture and a post-Christian West. In reality it simply follows Rousseau's lead. It points the finger of accusation against structures, traditions, rules, and dogma, imagining a kind of Christian "utopia of the picnic" where an idealized version of the early church becomes the benchmark. This industry conceives of the first movement as a kind of utopian community, pure and focused upon only the "essence" of Jesus' teachings. The term *radical,* often employed by those sitting in the place of critique, means a return to roots, back to this early Christian utopia. Rousseau believed that it was society that prevented us from returning to the happiness of the garden. In the bohemian Christian version, it is Christian culture that prevents us from returning to the utopian early church.

The problem with bohemia, both in its Christian and traditional forms, is that it does not match up with reality. Rousseau's belief that before society man lived blissfully in nature was formed upon sketchy and half-formed reports of tribal life. Rousseau would concoct the myth of the noble savage, the idea that non-Western people who lived outside of his definition of civilization were childlike and inherently good. This is a deeply racist and paternalistic view. Over time, as the field of anthropology grew, the West would discover that people who lived outside of "society" were in fact not necessarily moral or happy. Some tribal cultures were far more violent and dysfunctional than Western culture. Despite these realities, Rousseau's myth still remains strong in the Western mind. In the same way, the early church was not a peaceful, happy utopia. A quick reading of the New Testament letters reveals a dynamic yet often dysfunctional movement that was filled with all manner of human sin and brokenness, from self-interest, to false teaching, to sexual sins, to mistrust. Even in Jesus' discipleship community we find disbelief, self-interest, betrayal, and competition.

Sadly, Christian bohemians, whilst adept at pointing out structural and cultural sin, fail to notice their own sin. Jonah fails to notice that his shelter of religious protest and critique ultimately protects his own self-righteousness. Romanticism fumes against what it sees as the puritanism and pharisaicalness of mainstream culture, while ultimately remaining blind to the fact that it's entirely dependent upon embodying the very thing it ridicules. Ironically it was the Pharisees who were closest to Jesus' style of ministry. The zealots favored violent resistance to Roman rule. The Essenes had vacated the culture, attempting to rebuild a correct Judaism elsewhere, and the Sadducees had sold out to the dominant Hellenic culture. It was the Pharisees who were calling for Israel to return to

Scripture, to holiness, to prayer. They demanded that the people turn away from injustice and idolatry. Yet despite agreeing with so much of what Jesus spoke of, they wore their own radicalness and critique as a badge. The Pharisees found a sense of identity from broadcasting their redemptive acts. Like Jonah, they refused to see the ways in which God was working in the parts of the mainstream culture that they looked down upon. The critique, often containing elements of truth, becomes a protective position to hide behind. You will notice that leaders and influencers shaped by Romanticism will critique every inch of Christendom despite the fact that it is precisely this Christian kingdom that feeds and sustains their very own ministry success.

Christian bohemianism needs the Christian mainstream to sustain its own identity; it must define itself against it. Its attractiveness comes from the fact that it seems to offer an identity and social status to Christians who struggle to find these things in an increasingly secular culture that views religious belief with suspicion. This is seductive—particularly in a world in which the dominant social posture is one of hipness.

Camus noted that the bohemian's rebellion is a satanic impulse. The bohemian posture needs not only society to rebel against, but ultimately God. For Camus, the rebellion of the bohemian's ultimate ambition was "to talk to God as man to man."[13] It is this desire, and one of bohemianism's rotten fruits, that has spawned the "spiritual, not religious" subcategory, in that the individual chooses a pick-and-mix approach to faith whilst attempting to stare God in the eye as an equal. Those who believe that Christianity can be saved (as if it needed saving) and made relevant for the modern world by removing its structures, traditions, and dogmas, ultimately place the work of salvation in their own hands. If Rousseau is right, then Jesus did not need to die upon the cross and humans are inherently good. All Jesus had to do was to keep the good community vibes happening, keep the loaves and fish coming, avoid too many rules and strictures, and all would have been well.

Jonah's religious shelter of protest unwittingly becomes an attempt to depose God from His throne. Jonah knows better. In John Milton's poem "Paradise Lost," Satan, now in hell after being removed from heaven, declares to his fellow fallen angels, "Here at least we shall be free . . . Here we may reign secure . . . Better to reign in hell, than serve in heaven."[14] The bohemian mistaking of structures for sin ultimately only can destroy. To get back to the Christian utopia of the picnic, one must deconstruct, slash, and burn. The bohemian myth idolizes creativity, but ultimately it can only teach its disciples to destroy. The Christian utopia of the picnic, that Romanticism paints over the glorious, grace-filled messiness of the early church, was never Christian. It was always pagan. It was never centered around Christ but rather around other gods—Pan, Dionysius, Bacchae—the sophisticated grandchildren of the chaos monsters. It wore the garb of nature, of food, fun, and frivolity, yet under the picnic blanket, Leviathan always lurked.

Richard John Neuhaus warned that secularism has little interest in private faith. It was the institutions of religion that secularism wished to dismantle. When religion was "organized," it provided a "mediating structure—a community that generates and transmits moral values."[15] Without this mediating structure, all that is left is the power of the individual and of the state. The Christian utopia of the picnic, rebelling against all structure and systems, speeds up this process of secularization, joining in with secularism in promoting "spirituality" over and against "organized religion." The Christian utopia of the picnic sees sin as something that only exists in structures and systems, and sometimes it does. However, by holding on to Rousseau's vision the doctrine of Original Sin was, at best, downplayed and at its worst, forgotten. John Micklethwait and Adrian Wooldridge note that the rejection of Original Sin is the key that opens the door to secularism.[16] With the key turning, paganism could now reenter into the house it once owned.

PART VIII

A RETURN TO PAGANISM

The Rite *is a musical choreographic work . . . The piece has no plot.*

—IGOR STRAVINSKY on *The Rite of Spring*

A BALLET RIOT

The beautiful period of Parisian life is generally thought to have ended in the year 1914, scythed down by the outbreak of the Great War. One year before its demise, another kind of battle took place. This battle was not fought with guns and artillery but rather with music and dance. Combatants exchanged insults across the trenches of contemporary debate. The battle was the radical ballet *The Rite of Spring*. Now you probably have a lot of images in your mind when you think of ballet, but one thing that I am fairly sure does not spring to mind is riots. Yet for the Parisian audience at the premiere of *The Rite of Spring*, fights broke out in the audience.

Things had begun well. The Ballets Russes, the hottest dance company in the world, had made the journey from their base in St. Petersburg, exciting the Parisian cultural world with the promise of their latest offering. The respectable Parisians turned out in their formal regalia, and the progressives appeared in their bohemian wear: the scene was set for cultural war. The score written by the Russian composer Igor Stravinsky was radically new, taking musical history in a new direction. Rejecting all convention, it was starkly modern and grating to the ears of a nineteenth century audience reared on classical forms. Dance critic Judith Mackrell writes, "It twisted and compressed its sources into searing shapes and sounds. Rhythms splintered and collided, harmonies clashed, instruments played in pulsing, shrieking registers. If this was an evocation of spring, it was no gentle pastoral, but a season of cracking ice, violent wind and burning sun." Even more shocking was the choreography of Vaslav Nijinsky, which saw "Dancers in coarse tunics moved like peasants rather than princes and princesses: their shoulders were tense, their limbs awkwardly angled. They stamped, trembled and convulsed; when they jumped, they seemed hobbled by gravity, barely able to leave the floor. Protesters at the opening night shouted for a doctor, or even a dentist, given the convulsions of pain that seemed to afflict the dancers."[1]

According to media reports, members of the audience screamed. So chaotic was the response of the crowd that forty people were ejected from the theatre. The houselights were turned on and the show continued. As soon as the atonal music rang out, the audience began to voice its disapproval. This was met with cheers of approval from the bohemians in the audience who reveled in the taboo-smashing modernity of the performance. Fistfights broke out; there were rumors of duels fought the next morning. It was pandemonium. The line between spectator and performer had been crossed. The audience was now part of the performance.

EMOTIONS OVER REASON

One journalist sent to report on the performance got so caught up in the spectacle that reason gave way to sensation.

> I was sitting in a box in which I had rented one seat. Three ladies sat in front of me and a young man occupied the place behind me. He stood up during the course of the ballet to enable himself to see more clearly. The intense excitement under which he was laboring, thanks to the potent force of the music,

betrayed itself presently when he began to beat rhythmically on the top of my head with his fists. My emotion was so great that I did not feel the blows for some time. They were perfectly synchronised with the beat of the music. When I did, I turned around. His apology was sincere. We had both been carried beyond ourselves.[2]

The journalist and his fellow ballet fan's reaction to the play marked a new chapter in the insurgence of modernity. Western society was built upon a foundation of reason, yet this performance seemed to invoke a deeper, more primal response. This was a flight to raw emotions and feelings. This was Baudelaire's vision of art as life. This was art as revolution. If barricades and guns could not upturn society, discordant music and sporadic dancing could. The focus of the revolution had shifted from the economic to the moral.

Sexuality was central to *The Rite of Spring*. A narrative had begun, one that increased in volume during the nineteenth century, becoming deafening in the twentieth. This narrative told us that our sense of alienation, unhappiness, and anxiety stemmed from our lack of sexual liberation. Thus, Western culture would become obsessed with the traversing of sexual mores. It is telling that the victim of the pagan sacrifice in *The Rite of Spring* is a virginal young woman. Since the Middle Ages, the central character of sexual drama was the chaste young woman, untouched and untouchable, an idealized, saintly female symbolic of unrequited love, whom the Medieval troubadour could serenade. This was Shakespeare's Juliet and Dante's Beatrice. The whole cultural form of romance is built around this idealized female adoration and the various steps that the suitor must take to negotiate the traditions of courtship. Reflecting upon this older tradition, Dorothy L. Sayers notes that for us on this side of history, in which "the achievement of happiness has been erected into a moral obligation," the idea that we would deny ourselves sexual fulfillment seems unimaginable. However this was not always the

case. Before the modern period, those who were denied sexual fulfillment "suffered, no doubt, the usual bodily frustrations, but he
was not haunted by a guilty sense of personal failure and social in-
adequacy . . . nobody told him he was maladjusted, or hinted that
there was something seriously wrong with him if he was not up-
roariously releasing his repressions at every turn. On the contrary,
he was admired and commended. Whatever his private distresses,
he could feel that his public conduct was irreproachable. He was
sustained by his whole culture."[3]

Yet, by our day, such self-restraint was considered madness. Sexual
liberation has become one of the dominant ideologies of our time,
shaping all forms of contemporary discourse. Front and center of
The Rite of Spring is a sexually charged male, unconstrained, liberated
from the traditional covenantal codes that had surrounded sexuality.
Nijinksy in 1912 had shocked audiences with his sexually explicit
performance as a faun. Now the temper of how Western art viewed
human relationship would shift from the courtship of romance to
rebellion of unfettered eroticism. *The Rite of Spring* did not just sacrifice a virgin, it was the metaphorical sacrifice of virginity itself.

THE DEMI-MONDE

(Henri de Toulouse-Lautrec, *Alone*, 1896)

A companion piece to the sacrifice of the young woman in *The Rite of Spring* can be found in Henri de Toulouse-Lautrec's painting of an exhausted prostitute collapsed upon her bed. The painting is simply called *Alone*. Her client gone, she stares at the ceiling, trying to come back to her senses, almost crushed into her bed by the weight of the world. It is a picture over which hovers an aura of sadness. The picture is a counternarrative to Toulouse-Lautrec's more famous work in posters. These works celebrate the performative sexuality of the cancan and the provocative gyrations of Jane Avril, sex symbol and one of Paris's most famous dancers. Toulouse-Lautrec's poster of Avril shows her with one foot in the air in a time when women in public hid their heels. The hedonistic freedom of Avril stands in stark contrast to the heavy paralysis of the anonymous sex worker alone in her room.

Lautrec would become world-famous for cataloguing the sexual underbelly of Paris, known as the *demi-monde*, or half-world. This world of exploitation and objectification is the counterpoint to the myth of Paris as a capital of romance and entertainment. The government of Paris legalized prostitution, creating brothels, or as they were known then: "Houses of Tolerance." This turned Paris into Europe's capital of sex tourism in the second half of the nineteenth century. At its high point, a staggering 13 percent of Paris's population was engaged in the sex trade. This fact, alongside the growth of striptease in the city, led one commentator to label the city a pornocracy.

The conversion of the city into a locus of modern consumerism created an atmosphere of objectification. According to Aaron Betsky there seemed to be a connection between sex and shopping: "There was something promiscuous about the presentation of the goods that was matched with the availability of human bodies, and all of it could be surveyed by those men and women who were fortunate enough to have time for leisure."[4] This coupled with the bohemian desire to create a moral revolution, which upturned traditional views of marriage and sexuality, created a fertile ground for sexual exploitation. The bohemians and their sympathizers saw the traditional Christian view of sexuality as a restriction on individual freedom. They failed to see the ways in which traditional views of marriage actually protected women from being used and abused.

THE MORAL REVOLUTION

Stravinsky had returned to a past before the creation of the West, to the primitive—a theme that modernity would become obsessed with. This was Rousseau's "utopia of the picnic" but with a darker hue. In Manet's *Le déjeuner sur l'herbe*, the young naked woman in the garden would lose her clothes; in *The Rite of Spring*, she would lose her life, sacrificed to the primal chaotic forces. This was beyond bohemian posturing on a Saturday night at the Chat Noir, this was a moral revolution intent on destroying Western civilization. It was the creation of a new order through destruction. The hope was not to be found in the return to religious roots, "The theme was basic and at the same time brutal. If there was any hope, it was in the energy and fertility of life, not in morality. To an audience decked out in its civilized finery, the message was jarring."[5] The myth was bought. In order to create, first we must destroy.

In Baudelaire's manifesto, the poet notes that the bohemian male "makes the whole world his family, just like the lover of the fair sex who builds up his family from all the beautiful women that he has ever found, or that are—or are not—to be found."[6] Behind the florid language is a cutting idea. Eschewing traditional society and the middle-class family, the bohemian creates his own idealistic family. Community and family do not keep us rooted in reality, challenging the ego. Instead we are to pursue an idealistic communion with humanity—one that never impinges upon our will. Marriage is also removed from reality. Women are transformed from flesh and blood entities into ethereal objects of beauty, not demanding covenant but instead existing as visual stimulation. One of the great bohemian projects at the heart of Rousseau's revolution is the deconstruction of the natural family and the reshaping of marriage around the sexual desires of the male ego, which were no longer restrained and channeled by the institution of marriage. The social tradition of courtship leading to lifelong commitment is rejected; all that is left is unrestrained eros. Rousseau's reimagined garden contains no Adam or Eve, no creational order.

This rejection of the Christian idea of marriage, family, and the creational order was fundamental to bohemianism. Traditionally, experts have believed that the decline of marriage and the family follows after the decline of active Christian faith. The research of

Mary Eberstadt, however, paints a different picture. Eberstadt notes that in France, the decline of the family and marriage occurred at the same time as the decline of Christian faith. [7] The two factors operated in tandem. Bohemianism deconstruction of biblical models of human relationship created an open space for the rejection of Christian faith to take hold.

THE MORAL REVOLUTION BEGINS TO EAT THE WEST

As the twentieth century began, a cultural fear began to take hold of the West. Many wondered if the moral revolution had begun to destroy culture itself. Max Nordau's book *Degeneration* became a sensation, pointing the finger at Baudelaire and bohemianism. Nordau saw the bohemian culture as a destructive force within the West. As the century ended, an apocalyptic atmosphere began to infect the air. The artists and the writers still proclaimed bohemian mantras, but the politicians, the industrialists, and the generals began to prepare for war. Nordau, a German-speaking Hungarian of Jewish descent, sensed that a storm was brewing in Europe. He advised his fellow Jews to leave behind the Continent and to return to Israel.

THE WANDERING BIRDS

At the beginning of the twentieth century you could find groups of young people wandering through the German countryside. These young people called themselves *Wandervogel* (wandering birds), and they longed for a life away from the suburbs and the cities, to find themselves again in nature. Turned off by consumerism, industry, and social convention, they took to the countryside to discover and model a different vision of life. "We were something like a protest against the bourgeois world . . . It was a spiritual movement,"[8] remembers Bruno Hahnel who would, like so many others, move from membership in the Wandervogel to the Nazi party.

The Wandervogel was more a movement than an organization. Jon Savage writes, "Their young adherents felt that the only way forward was backward: into the paganism of nature worship. However, in seeking to cast off adult restraints, they left themselves open to the demons lying beneath the ordered, apparently rational surface of European life."[9] In many ways the wandering birds were living out the utopia of the picnic, carrying on the tradition of bohemianism. They believed in *Jugendkultur*, or youth culture—a generation gap and a rebellion against parental influence and authority. They believed in intellectual freedom and they wanted to wander through the countryside and sit by a fire with a copy of Nietzsche. The wandering birds are seen by many as the first kernels of the homosexual rights movement. Authors attached to the movement, such as Hans Bluher and William Jansen, advocated a return to the ancient Greek idea of homosexual patronage, in which older boys would form sexual relationships with younger boys. The wandering birds were also attracted to more esoteric spiritualities, a worship of the body, and physical fitness. They preferred folk music to middle-class musical tastes. They desired community of authentic relationships over a society built upon commercial and formal relationships—all values that seem progressive in our day, causing a number of cultural historians to see the wandering birds as a precursor to the hippie movement of the 1960s.

Yet there was something else going on. Karl Fischer, one of the leaders of the movement, was addressed as *Führer*. Members greeted each other with a *Heil*. Fischer would speak of young people needing a *lebensraum* or living space to live out this bohemian life—a term later used by Adolf Hitler to justify the invasion of Eastern Europe. This was more than just disorganized French bohemians, this was now a movement centered on the "utopia of the picnic."

GERMANY RISING

Germany at the onset of World War I saw itself as the world's first truly modern people, a people with a mission, an alternative to the bourgeois middle classes of France and Britain. Germany's enemies lampooned her people as mechanical, stiff, and unimaginative, but Germans saw themselves as sincere, vibrant, and creative. A people chosen by history, who had now arrived on the world stage. "In the international context Germans were inclined to regard their country as a progressive, liberating force," writes Modris Eckstein, who notes that just as in *The Rite of Spring*, undergirding this mission was a "fascination with primitivism, or, in another sense, the desire to establish contact with the elemental in the German spirit, reached many levels in Germany, particularly within the middle classes . . . with its urge to escape from an urban civilization of mere form and sham back into nature."[10] It meant liberation from middle-class life at every level. Germany was at the forefront of cultural change; a clean break with the recent past was in the making. The modes that had guided everything from religion to sexuality, to art and society, were to be deconstructed and rebuilt from the ground up. Unsurprisingly, whereas outrage and catcalls had greeted *The Rite of Spring* in Paris, Sergei Diaghilev, founder of the Ballets Russes, recorded that German audiences were more enthusiastic of his freedom-spouting work.

Germany, more than any other country, would shape the organic values. It was the home of the Protestant Reformation, of Martin Luther, who, driven by personal conviction and faith, stood up to the Catholic authorities and held firm to his ideals. As German culture developed, this willingness to challenge authority lost its Christian kernel but remained part of their national identity. The forms of Christian discipleship mutated into a secular form. Thus, in contrast to the superficialities and faddishness of French Romanticism, the German version of Romanticism is idealistic, serious, and determined. The German romanticist is an artistic, engaged visionary, moving toward emotional maturity, creative freedom, and expression. The German model of life was able to combine success and artistic creativity as possible. The creative was a leader and an influencer, a world changer. History, revelation, and ethics were ditched for ideals, essence, and vitalism. The groundwork was set for German liberal theologians who ripped Christ from His historical context, reinventing him as a Hegelian agent of change. Judaism and Christianity rooted in history became problematic in this new vision. The historicity of the gospel and the life, death, and resurrection of Christ had acted as a bulwark in Western culture's attempt to return to pagan self-worship. However, with the advent of liberal theology and the rise of the organic values in Germany, this bulwark was being dismantled.

In 1834 the poet Heinrich Heine had prophetically written of his people,

> Christianity . . . has somewhat mitigated that brutal German love of war, but it could not destroy it. Should that subduing talisman, the cross, be shattered, the frenzied madness of the ancient warriors, that insane Berserk rage of which Nordic bards have spoken and sung so often, will once more burst into flame. Then the ancient stony gods will rise from the forgotten debris and rub the dust of a thousand years from their eyes, and finally Thor with his giant hammer will jump up and smash the Gothic cathedral . . . When you hear a crashing such as never before has been heard in the world's history, then you will know that the German thunderbolt has fallen at last. At that uproar the eagles of the air will drop dead . . . A play will be performed in Germany that will make the French Revolution look like an innocent idyll.[11]

Germany and modernism were preparing the ground for a return to paganism. Modernism seemed to be a cult of the new, but at its heart was a desire to return to the pre-Christian classical culture of Greece and Rome, a reaching back behind the culture of Christianity. No country had pursued this agenda as strongly as Germany, be it a return to Greek pagan ideals or an embrace of the pagan culture and gods of pre-German history. Heine was right: a stage was being set for a terrible play the likes of which the world had never experienced.

Six years after the Parisian premiere of *The Rite of Spring*, Germany began what would be the Great War, and sixteen million young European lives would be sacrificed like the lone young woman in Stravinsky's ballet. Most would be buried in mass graves. A further twenty million would be wounded. Countless would return fit in body but wounded in mind. Those who had demanded that society be ripped down in order to return to the vital soil of paganism seemed to have their wish fulfilled by the carnage of World War I. "It reversed the idea of progress,"[12] notes author Paul Fussell. The unbridled enthusiasm in humanity's potential was left behind in the trenches of World War I.

PARIS EXPOSITION UNIVERSELLE 1937

A new landmark now stood out in the Parisian cityscape, a radiant cathedral of light that punctured the darkness. At night the beams of light that shot up from the building stole all attention away from the Eiffel Tower. In the day the building was even more spectacular, a defiant architectural statement to the world. Whereas in previous Expositions, nations had fought for prime positions, pushing their national brand over others, the 1937 Paris World Exposition was different. The German pavilion fought an architectural war. The pavilion featured spotlights that gave the effect at night of the building reaching transcendently into the heavenlies. A Nazi swastika and an eagle adorned the building.

It was a remarkable turnaround. A hero had seemingly appeared. At the beginning of Leni Riefenstahl's groundbreaking documentary of the Nazi rallies at Nuremberg, Hitler is shown descending from the sky in an airplane like a conquering hero, a sky hero, who had vanquished the cultural storms that had descended upon Germany, who had redeemed the chaos and shame of Germany's defeat in World War I, and who had appeared to reverse the collapse of the German economy in the wake of the global depression. A new spring had seemingly been birthed.

BALANCING THE HERO AND THE CHAOS MONSTER

In his work *The Birth of Tragedy*, Friedrich Nietzsche attempted to fuse the chaotic with the heroic, to hold the sky hero in perfect tension with the chaos monster of the deep. Nietzsche believed that Christianity and the morality it established had ruined the West. The remedy was to mimic the way that the ancient pagan Greeks had held in tension the chaotic and ecstatic with the ordered and the restrained. According to Nietzsche, the operas of Richard Wagner captured this balance. Hitler's worldview would be deeply formed by the work of Wagner and thus, Nazism would mimic a balance between the chaotic and the heroic. Germany, famed for its efficiency and order, would be presided over by a leader attempting to live out a Romantic—yet deadly—vision of life.

Hitler understood that it was his role as Führer to play the hero. Telling his propaganda minister Joseph Goebbels, "Only through a heroic attitude can we survive this hardest of times,"[13] Hitler portrayed a public image almost unparalleled in history. Every element of his public self was consumed with communicating the supreme ideal of leadership. Hitler intuitively understood the age of the image, believing that the public would willingly trade in democracy for "bread and circuses." Hitler and his public relations team were keen students of the American advertising industry, in particular of ad man Edward Bernays, the nephew of Sigmund Freud. Bernays used his uncle's methods to sell products to the public and the public's desire to break free from tradition and convention. He famously encouraged women to see the smoking of cigarettes as a weapon in the battle for gender equality. Using the techniques of public relations, as well as emerging communication techniques, Hitler became a brand, a symbol of godlike power, creating in his followers a cult-like devotion. In public he was a highly disciplined actor playing out a role, taking utter care with every element of his performance. This is the Hitler we know; the ordered dictator of a mechanical, totalitarian regime.

THE BOHEMIAN DICTATOR

Yet away from the public, a radically different Hitler appears. Those surrounding Hitler dealt with a very different individual, a man who embodied chaos. The ludicrous reality of the Nazi regime consisted of confused subordinates trying to get a hold of their chaotic and indolent leader; subordinates who ultimately tried to run the country in the way that they believed would please their publicly rigid, mechanical Führer. However, even as leader of Germany, Hitler lived the life of a nineteenth-century bohemian. Prominent Hitler historian Ian Kershaw notes that virtually nothing changes in Hitler's lifestyle from when he was an art school drifter in Vienna to when he was dictator of Germany and half of Europe. One colleague believed he was the combination of a military man and a creative artist. His friend Putzi Hanfstaengl recalled him as "a bohemian whose unreliability drove his colleagues to despair."[14] Leading

Germany, he would avoid paperwork and organization. Staying up into the small hours of the morning and rising late in the day, he preferred to work from cafes, studios, and restaurants. Meals rather than meetings were the axis points of the working day.

He could not stand politicians. His friend Albert Speer remembered that he would launch into "tirades about his everlasting struggle against the idiocy of the bureaucracy." He would repeatedly lament "that he had become a politician against his will, that basically he was an architect."[15] He loved movies. Even during the difficult days of the war, cinema was always a priority—every night movies were put on for Hitler and his entourage.

He followed trends that had developed in Germany around diet and health, avoiding alcohol and tobacco and advocating vegetarianism. Like a good German Romantic, he enjoyed nature walks and mountain vistas. His lair atop a mountain at Obersalzberg gave him a view of the world that seemed to mimic German painter Caspar David Friedrich's classic work *The Wanderer*, which had regained popularity during the Nazi period. Following the bohemian template, he avoided marriage, only wedding on the eve of his suicide, a last-minute act of gratitude to his girlfriend, Eva Braun. His entourage was a collection of outliers and social misfits, ranging from the neo-pagan Heinrich Himmler to the homosexual standover man Ernst Röhm. His overriding vision for Germany was totally Romantic in nature. The eastern lands would be conquered and resettled by Germans who would live out communal lives, working off the land, closely in touch with nature and "the soil." It was the dream of the wandering birds writ large.

Nazi Germany became a giant Romantic society of the spectacle. Raw emotion now ruled over reason. So deep was the cult of creativity that Speer recalls that Hitler was more upset by the destruction of theaters and opera houses than he was of human lives.[16] Life had become an absurd theatre. Hitler was its most consummate actor. The line between stage and audience, punctured in Paris at the premiere of *The Rite of Spring*, was now broken. Bohemianism as devised by Baudelaire was ultimately a form of urban acting, of living life as art. "To live and die before a mirror" was Baudelaire's slogan, notes Albert Camus. Reflecting in the wake of the war upon the bohemian posture, Camus writes,

> Up to now, man derived his coherence from the Creator. But from the moment that he consecrates his rupture from Him, he finds himself delivered over to the fleeting moment, to the passing days, and to wasted sensibility. Like all people without a rule of life, he is only coherent as an actor. He can only be sure of his own existence by finding it in the expression of others' faces. Other people are his mirror. A mirror that quickly becomes clouded. Perpetually incomplete, he compels others to create him, while denying their values. He plays at life because he is unable to live it.[17]

Thus we can understand why after over a thousand words of exploration and description, Hitler's biographer Ian Kershaw writes that Hitler "was tantamount to an unperson."[18] And why Modris Eksteins declares, "At the center there was nothing, an utter vacuum. Only an audience could give Hitler meaning; he had none himself."[19] Thus he must continue to create. Hitler dreamed of rebuilding Berlin as a city of beauty and creativity that would outshine Paris. He would build even bigger boulevards and opera houses than Hausmann. As one Nazi motto proclaimed, "The German everyday shall be beautiful." With emotion overtaking reason, with Christianity and Judaism being superseded by German neo-paganism, with the vigor and vitality of modernism no longer held back by convention, ethics, and justice, Leviathan was no longer restrained. The hero and the chaos monster had fused. Nietzsche had proclaimed that the heir to the open space created by the death of God would be a new breed of hero-men who come like light-ning out of the storm. And thus out of Nazi Germany would pour *Sturmtruppen*, literally "storm soldiers," who would wage *Blitzkreig*, lightning war, upon the world.

For Hitler's "utopia of the picnic" to be realized in the East, there had to be a cost. Volumes of books have been filled listing the Nazi atrocities. We could point to the purges within Germany against political enemies, the "euthanizing" of the mentally ill and disabled, the death camps and concentration camps filled with mangled corpses, the carpet-bombing of cities. Goebbels, Hitler's master of spin, had written in excitement, "Under the debris of the cities, the last so-called achievements of the middle-class nineteenth century have been buried."[20] The great modernist myth of creativity had told us that to achieve a world of beauty, self-expression, and authenticity, first we must destroy; in order to beat Leviathan, the hero must discover the chaos within them. Yet now according to Ecksteins, chaos and destruction were in the ascendancy, "The urge to create and the urge to destroy changed places. The urge to destroy was intensified; the urge to create became increasingly abstract. In the end the abstractions turned to insanity and all that remained was destruction."[21]

Soon it would be Hitler that would be under siege. His Berlin transformed not into his vision of an ungraded Paris, but rather into a landscape of utter obliteration. Beneath the city, now rat-like, Hitler would spend his last days delusional, narcissistic, and eventually suicidal. The final act of the horrifying underground drama of the bunker takes place not with the suicide of Hitler, but with the act of Joseph Goebbels, who had boasted that middle-class culture would ultimately die under the ruins of the cities. Goebbels and his wife would commit a brutally vicious act of the Nazi regime, killing the ultimate symbol of middle-class convention: the family. Goebbels killed his six children before shooting his wife and then himself. The Jewish Torah, which the Nazis took delight in burning, had warned that ultimately the chaos monster would want us to sacrifice our children. The Torah was right.

PART IX

LEADER ON A CROSS

The moral decay of imperial Rome was overcome by the gospel for that day, and the moral decay of Western civilization will be likewise overcome by the gospel for our day.

—ELTON TRUEBLOOD, *The Predicament of Modern Man*

CREATIVITY OUTSIDE OF THE CREATED ORDER

When writing a book such as this, one can be thrown into another kind of abyss. A sea of books, a storm of facts, ideas, and theories. Spending every waking hour solving problems that your work throws at you, a distance grows between you and others. The normalities of life begin to fade as more books cover the floor of your office and as ideas fill your mind. A book like this, focusing upon history, can transport your mental landscape back in time. One morning, however, I left behind my books, got into my car, and drove to the Holocaust Museum.

The Holocaust Museum in Melbourne is not large. Situated in a small side street in a predominantly Jewish neighborhood, you could easily miss it. It's a weekday midmorning. The school groups have not arrived yet, and apart from the staff, the museum seems empty. I walk up to the first display. It is a collection of photos; most feature a teenage boy. There are family snaps, those mementoes that we take to mark the occasions of life. The photos illustrate the life of what looks like a fairly normal middle-class Jewish family living their lives in prewar Poland. The story of this young man's life accompanies the photos. The initial persecution of Jews, the transportation to the camps, then the death of his entire family. The progression in the photos from the happy family in peacetime to those of the death camps exemplifies so much of the question that hangs over the twentieth century, over the culture of the West. How did supposedly enlightened Europe get from the first photo to the second? This theoretical question fades into the back of my mind as I continue to follow the story of the boy in the death camps. The sheer injustice, the cost, the tragedy of it all begin to hit me. As I stand staring at the photos, trying to keep a lid on my emotions, I am wrenched from the moment as a voice behind me says, "Hello." Annoyed at this interruption, I turn around. A small but fit-looking old man stands behind me, his hands folded together in front of him. I look at the man, fake a smile, and prepare to rebuff his interruption. Then a spark of recognition comes over me. His face looks familiar. Do I know him? I look again at the photo on the wall. The old man smiles. He is the boy in the photos.

I feel an incredible sense of dislocation for a second. No longer am I immersed in theory, buried in books, lost in photos. This is not history; this is a living human being. Again the old man kindly smiles and asks, "Would you like to ask me anything?" My mind goes into hyper-speed trying to find something meaningful to ask him that will measure up to the profundity of his lived experience. That horrible pride in me files through all of the theories, facts, and history, trying to clutch on to a deep and meaningful question, as I want to appear smart. I realize I am not talking to a professor, an expert, an author, or a commentator. I am speaking to a witness. My question seems so cliché, probably because it is the question that our hearts rather than our heads want to know. Defeated, I simply ask, "What was it like?" The old man walks with me through the displays of the museum and tells me his story. Nothing is rote nor mechanical. He tells me of the different camps in which he lived, of what it was to work in them. As he describes his eventual liberation by British troops, his emotions are palpable. A school group enters the museum, and my guide politely bids me farewell to attend to the group, no doubt again quietly telling the group his story.

As I walk out of the museum onto the ordinary street outside, I realize that somehow our conversation illuminated the twisted trajectory of Western thought and leadership. As soon as that man greeted me, I was confronted with a person, not an image—a story, not a theory. Our society of the spectacle reduced people to images. It turned its back upon a foundational biblical truth: when we encounter another, we encounter the image of God.

Out of all the people in the world God chose the Jews. He called them apart, withdrawing them from the pagan sea that surrounded them, teaching them to follow Him in the everyday, in lived history. They were called not to the idea of justice but to justice itself. God demanded of them not a theory of righteousness but to be righteous. He called them not to create images but to reflect His image. Out of this people would one day come a Messiah who would heal the world.

Yet the followers of the Messiah in the early church and today eventually forget. The allure of paganism proves overwhelming. Yes, there would be your Dietrich Bonhoeffers and Corrie ten Booms, but far too many would fall for the sirens, the tyrant, the pagan hero. Abraham Heschel, an advocate of biblical leadership writing in the midst of a Nazi Germany that had fallen for Hitler's spell, would note that the biblical leader's mind "is preoccupied with man, with the concrete actualities of history rather than with the timeless issues of thought . . . He is one not only with what he says; he is involved with his people in what his words foreshadow . . . his life and soul are at stake in what he says and in what is going to happen to what he says."[1]

BIBLICAL LEADERSHIP IS SO MUCH MORE THAN JUST LEADING PEOPLE. THE BIBLICAL LEADER IS A SYMBOL WHO LIVES AT THE INTERSECTION OF GOD'S BREAKING INTO HISTORY, INTO LIFE. THE LEADER CAN NEVER BE DISTANT FROM GOD, HIS WORD, OR THE WORLD.

DISTANT GOD, DISTANT PROPHET

Jonah continued to sit, maintaining his religious critique of God and Nineveh. He could not allow his heart to go out to Nineveh's citizens, acknowledging them as brothers and sisters also made in the image of God. He could not overcome his "reasonable" frustration with God for allowing this rotten city to repent in such a painless way in comparison to his own nation's grueling struggle to do so. His story continues:

> Then the Lord God provided a leafy plant and made it grow up over Jonah to give shade for his head to ease his discomfort, and Jonah was very happy about the plant. But at dawn the next day God provided a worm, which chewed the plant so that it withered. When the sun rose, God provided a scorching east wind, and the sun blazed on Jonah's head so that he grew faint. He wanted to die, and said, "It would be better for me to die than to live." (Jonah 4:5–8)

Obviously Jonah's self-constructed sukkah is insufficient. God's Word again comes at Jonah through an east wind. The Hebrew word *ruach* used to describe this wind is the same word used for the wind of the storm sent to Jonah at sea. Again it is Jonah, not Nineveh, who is convicted and torn apart by God. Jonah came as an agent and partner with God to convict Nineveh of their self-serving agenda. Yet as God speaks, it is Jonah's agenda that is revealed.

> But God said to Jonah, "Is it right for you to be angry about the plant?" "It is," he said. "And I'm so angry I wish I were dead." But the Lord said, "You have been concerned about this plant, though you did not tend it or make it grow. It sprang up overnight and died overnight. And should I not have concern for the great city of Nineveh, in which there are more than a hundred and twenty thousand people who cannot tell their right hand from their left—and also many animals?" (Jonah 4:9–10)

After the drama of the storm at sea, the miraculous conversion of Nineveh, and Jonah's protest to God, the book shudders to an abrupt halt. What happens to Jonah? What happens to Nineveh?

What is Jonah's reply? The book ends with silence. It is not the silence of God. Rather the exclamation mark at the end of this book is the passivity, the distance, the inability of Jonah to reply. We are left wondering what happened to the nationwide conversion occurring in Nineveh. This silence continues throughout the Bible. What has happened to the great pagan capital that turned to the Lord? What happened to the possibility of Israel having an ally in following God? All we have is the denunciations against the city found in Nahum and Zephaniah. God's last words are illuminating. He makes deliberate mention of the citizens of Nineveh, "who cannot tell their right hand from their left." This statement refers to the Ninevites before they repented and called upon the Lord, but the statement also speaks of a pagan people who have found God and who need instruction, who need a prophet to dwell amongst them—someone from the chosen nation who can teach them how to follow God. Nineveh, after its conversion from paganism, will need a leader like Elisha who during a destructive reign of kings created a company of prophets to rebuild the shattered religious and cultural terrain. Instead, the last image of the book of Jonah leaves us with the reluctant prophet remaining stationary, unable to leave his self-constructed religious shelter of protest, unable to sacrifice his own agenda and pride.

In the same way, our own Christian versions of bohemia—our self-constructed religious spaces of critique—cannot save. Mumford notes that while the bohemian position wanted to retain the "Christian impulse of love . . . they failed to retain the co-ordinate doctrine of sacrifice."[2] Jonah's story teaches us that heroic actions of leaders ultimately cannot save. Neither can bohemian-flavored critical distance from the world. Despite their best efforts, both lead to violence and chaos. They undo the world. The silence of Jonah left a vacuum into which only a different kind of leadership could enter. The space was now open for a leadership of sacrifice.

THE CHAOS MONSTER DEFEATED

While Jonah would remain distant from the world of Nineveh, caught in his theory of critique, God would come close. He models His own leadership. In the Old Testament, God was dominant over the forces of chaos. Psalm 74 exclaims,

> It was you who split open the sea by your power;
>   you broke the heads of the monster in the waters.
> It was you who crushed the heads of Leviathan.
> (Psalm 74:13–14)

God's ability to triumph over Leviathan, to control the chaos that threatens to overtake the world, is never in doubt. God is Israel's hero. The rabbis would speak of a feast that would occur when the Messiah would heroically arrive to rule from Jerusalem, placing the nations under the feet of Israel. At that feast a dish would be served. God, having defeated Leviathan, would serve the chaos monster to His people. Yet His people distanced from Him by sin feel at times as though the chaos will overtake them. Psalm 69 cries out,

> Save me, O God,
>   for the waters have come up to my neck.
> I sink in the miry depths,
>   where there is no foothold.
> I have come into the deep waters;
>   the floods engulf me.
> I am worn out calling for help;
>   my throat is parched.
> My eyes fail,
>   looking for my God.

Cursing the day he was born, Job wishes for Leviathan to be roused, for the sinful world to be again undone by chaos.

May gloom and utter darkness claim it once more;
    may a cloud settle over it;
    may blackness overwhelm it.
That night—may thick darkness seize it;
    may it not be included among the days of the year
    nor be entered in any of the months.
May that night be barren;
    may no shout of joy be heard in it.
May those who curse days curse that day,
    those who are ready to rouse Leviathan. (Job 3:5–8)

Unlike Jonah, God cannot remain distant. He humbles Himself, trading His throne in heaven for a cross on earth. The God who comes in a storm becomes fully human. His life on earth is not filled with heroic acts of bravery and grandeur. Incredibly, much of His life on earth is hidden in the obscurity of the mundane. After being baptized He withdraws into the wilderness, facing Satan who tempts Him to use His power by quoting Psalm 91.

"He will command his angels concerning you,
    and they will lift you up in their hands,
    so that you will not strike your foot against a stone."
(Matthew 4:6)

Satan stops short, failing to quote the next part of the Psalm that reads, "You will tread on the lion and the cobra; you will trample the great lion and the serpent" (Psalm 91:13). The serpent mentioned here is from the Hebrew *tannin*, meaning a serpent, dragon, or sea monster.

The serpent will be trampled. The chaos monster of the deep will be defeated. Victory will not come, however, from an act of pagan heroism, from a moment of redemptive violence in which a man becomes a god. Rather God becomes a man. Humans could never defeat chaos, because the chaos was in us. When we attempted to heroically battle chaos monsters, we became them. When we tried to deconstruct our way back to the garden, to the utopia of the picnic, our own selfishness blocked our way. Utopia becomes dystopia. On a hill named skull, where the refuse of Jerusalem lay, creation held its breath, as the ultimate battle with chaos occurred. However, this time everything was different. The God who came with lightning and power on a cloud left behind His royal garb and instead was clothed in naked humanity.

It was a *chaoskampf,* a battle between good and evil, between creation and destruction. Yet at the moment when the God was meant to triumph, there was no flashing sword, no heavenly army. The sea did not froth and bubble as a muscular hero fought with superhuman strength. Instead of triumphant cries, there was only an anguished shout as God exclaims from dying lungs, "My God, my God, why have you forsaken me?" (Mark 15:34).

The God who comes on clouds in victory unbelievably now is in free fall. God descends into *Sheol,* the place of the dead, drowning in the sea of destruction, engulfed by the jaws of Leviathan. The fabric in the curtain of the temple that symbolized the separation not only of the holiest of the holies but of the land and the sea, the boundary that holds back the chaos, is torn from top to bottom. The abyss seemingly now breaks into the world as the graves give up bodies, as the dead walk amongst the living. The raw materials of our world shudder and break. Light, the first act of creation representing the first words of God that spring creation into being, appears to be undone as darkness covers the land.

God is dead. Chaos is unmaking the world. Leviathan has surely won.

In the darkness, a spark of light arose from an unlikely source. A Roman centurion, cloaked in the armor of the heroic myth, utters from his pagan lips, "Surely he was the Son of God!" (Matthew 27:54).

Yet this spark is the only illumination for three dark days. The world is not unmade. The seas had not dried up. The stars had not fallen out of the sky. Life continues, yet everything had changed. A revolution had begun. God had defeated chaos. Leviathan was beaten. God had taken the chaos and sin that exists in the human heart upon Himself. Like Jonah, He had plunged into the abyss as a sacrifice. Yet unlike Jonah, He would not remain distant. He must withdraw, but He will return.

THE DEATH OF THE PAGAN HERO

The bumbling crew that was Jesus' disciples often fought for prominence, scrapping and squabbling with each other as to who would sit at His right hand. Their continual following of Jesus shows their belief in and appreciation of His teachings. They were prepared to back Him to the hilt . . . except when He spoke of what was going to happen—of how He must die. Upon such words the disciples' indignation would rise. It clashed with their deeply entrenched idea that God's victory in the world would be won with heroic, powerful, and violent grandeur. It would result in them being lifted up, triumphant over the nations. Yet if they had watched and listened, Jesus was living out a completely different way of leading. He had taught them, "You know that the rulers of the Gentiles lord it over them, and their high officials exercise authority over them. Not so with you. Instead, whoever wants to become great among you must be your servant, and whoever wants to be first must be your slave— just as the Son of Man did not come to be served, but to serve, and to give his life as a ransom for many" (Matthew 20:25–28).

On the cross, God does not just die. The myth of the heroic pagan god who will save us through a kind of earthly power, rooted in revenge and domination also dies. Instead the God who leads by serving, saves by dying.

SACRIFICIAL LOVE, WRAPPED UP IN GRACE, IS WHAT SAVES. THE POWER WITH WHICH GOD TRIUMPHS OVER THE ABYSS, SIN, CHAOS, AND DEATH IS A POWER MADE PERFECT IN WEAKNESS.

The rabbis had speculated that at the feast at the end of the age, the righteous will feast upon the flesh of Leviathan. Yet Jesus tells His disciples to eat of His body, to drink of His blood. It is a stunning turnaround. The apostle Paul, once himself on a heroic, violent, and misguided mission to serve God is brought to his knees, humbled on his way to Syria. Later, understanding the revolution in leadership that God has brought into the world tells those who make up the first rumblings of the Jesus movement not to follow the pagan path of the hero, boasting of one's glory, but rather "boast all the more gladly about my weaknesses, so that Christ's power may rest on me" (2 Corinthians 12:9).

The hero of mythology descends from the sky, gaining fame and glory through courage, violence, and power. He then dies, His grave becoming a sight of hero worship. Christ defies this cycle. He emerges from the tomb, remaking the world with resurrection power, ascending to heaven because of His humility, His servant leadership. After Jesus' death and resurrection, the world would never be the same. Those who bow their knee at the foot of the cross admitting the absurdity of their own efforts to be godlike, who confess the chaos and sin within them, now enter into a new way of being—one not driven by striving, agenda, or applause. For these followers of Jesus would be taught to follow this new way of living and leading:

> Do nothing out of selfish ambition or vain conceit. Rather, in humility, value others above yourselves, not looking to your own interests but each of you to the interests of the others.
> In your relationships with one another, have the same mind-set as Christ Jesus:
> Who, being in very nature God,
>   did not consider equality with God something to be used
> to his own advantage;
>   rather, he made himself nothing
>   by taking the very nature of a servant,
>   being made in human likeness.
>   And being found in appearance as a man,
>   he humbled himself
>   by becoming obedient to death—
>   even death on a cross!
>   Therefore God exalted him to the highest place
>   and gave him the name that is above every name. (Philippians 2:3–9)

However it would not only be the heroic mode of leading and living that would be undone by Jesus' death upon the cross. Those who wished to side with chaos, who wished to build by first tearing down, would also find that Jesus' death changes the way we view creativity and chaos.

CREATIVITY AND CHAOS

The cross shows that there doesn't always have to be destruction in order to create. God as the ultimate Creator must, in a sense, withdraw in order to create. In order to create, He permits spaces in which His will is not pursued to its fullest. He allows humans and angels the terrible liberty of free will. This allowance creates the possibility of chaos and the potential of evil. Thus fittingly an act of destruction occurs.

In one sense, those who follow the Romantic, bohemian path are correct: to create, we must destroy and create chaos. Yet, because we are not God, we cannot hold back the chaos. It is too powerful for us. Ultimately once we erase those God-given boundaries that hold back the chaos, we unleash the chaos monsters in ourselves. We are left with one of the great problems not just for the creative leader but for humanity. How do we create without being overtaken by the chaos that creativity brings? The cross answers this conundrum conclusively. To create, God must allow chaos. The first image of the Bible in Genesis is of the Spirit hovering over the unformed chaotic ocean, and Leviathan dwells in God's created sea. However chaos surges and resists being imprisoned; it rebels against God. However, chaos cannot defeat chaos. To re-create the world, Jesus takes the chaos of the world upon Himself.

A REVOLUTION IN THE SOCIETY OF THE SPECTACLE

The Roman society of the spectacle, built upon grand processions, resplendent temples, and gory entertainment, barely noticed what had changed under its feet. Off in the backwater of Israel, in an upper room, people transformed by the Servant King, powered by the Spirit, tumbled out of the darkness and into the street. Their own compatriots laughed at them, calling them drunkards (Acts 2).

Slowly spilling out, across the empire, one life at a time, a rumbling, rolling revolution was breaking out. It did not happen in the spotlight, it was not thrilling or spectacular—at least in the way that the pagan mind understood it. It seemed to exist in the dark, underground places: in the quietness of rooms, catacombs, and the ordinariness of life. Yet there was nothing ordinary about it. Victor Hugo writes, "The Darkness, that murky incubator of primitive Christianity, was just waiting for the chance to set off an explosion under the Caesars and flood the human race with light. For in the thickest darkness there is latent light. Volcanoes are full of darkness capable of bursting into flame. All lava begins in blackness. The catacombs, where the first mass was said, were not only the caves of Rome, they were the underground of the world."[3]

In the wake of the Servant King's death and resurrection, everything had changed. The stratified society of the ancient world, built upon power and violence was sent into a sprawling confusion by this new way of living. Imagine the shock of a powerful Roman man who has just discovered Christ. A man of means who had served in the military rose up the ranks, spending his life giving orders to soldiers and slaves. Imagine his shock, the ignominy of sitting down to a meal next to a slave girl from a foreign land. Of having to break the bread, drink the wine with such a lowly person, having to converse with her as a sister in Christ, sitting together listening to the apostles teaching, hearing a letter from Paul that scandalously claims, "There is neither Jew nor Gentile, neither slave nor free, nor is there male and female, for you are all one in Christ Jesus" (Galatians 3:28).

Such a man would sit and wonder how on earth he could tell his friends about this new truth. How could such a message be made relevant to the Roman world—a world built upon the myth of Romulus, a hero raised by a wolf, who kills and leads, steals women, and creates Rome out of sheer will and authoritarian power? And yet the message did spread, moving beyond the border of the Greco-Roman world, reaching into our day. It truly was a revolution.

A NEW UNDERSTANDING OF THE MODERN WORLD

When we understand that Christ's sacrificial mode of loving, living, and leading was a revolution that overturned the pagan world, we gain a new understanding of those "turning points" in Western history such as the Renaissance and the Enlightenment, which were essentially attempts to return to the pagan order. The term Renaissance means rebirth, a rebirth that began when scholars began looking at pagan philosophy as the prime guidance in life. Our history tells us that the modern world began when Italian scholars of the fifteenth century again discovered text like Lucretius's "On the Nature of Things," a poem that painted a world distant from God, a random universe in which humans must shape lives of meaning and pleasure. Again we are back in the pagan world, the fusion of order and chaos, the melding of the hero and the genius. Modernity wears the cloak of the new. Its creed is one of destruction; it is perpetual revolution, a never-ending quest for liberty and freedom. Yet at its heart, modernity is an attempt to wind back the clock, to return to a pre-Christian dawn. It is a saccharine repainting of classical paganism. There is nothing new about it. It is a desire to return to the past. Theologian David Bentley Hart writes, "It is my governing conviction . . . that much of modernity should be understood not as a grand revolt against the tyranny of faith, not as a movement of human liberation and progress, but as a counter-revolution, a reactionary rejection of a freedom that it no longer understands, but upon which it remains parasitic."[4]

Our modern world is not so modern after all. Rather it is a return to paganism. In paganism one could manipulate the gods through offerings, prayers, and incantations. The idols, made in the image of their own creators, were really always just extensions of the individual. In the pagan universe, the desires and wishes of the individual remained triumphant. Christianity turned everything in the pagan order around. It was a cultural revolution in a Greco-Roman world built not only upon power, order, and violence, but also debauchery, exploitation, and the spectacle. Into this world, Christianity's teachings exploded because the people, especially the sexually exploited women and slaves, found Christian belief liberating. It restrained male eros and elevated the value of the women and slaves to more than just how many children they could bear or how much sexual pleasure they could provide.

Christianity does not ask that we remove the heroic, the instinct within us to change the world, the part of us that desires to courageously risk for a greater good. Nor does Christianity ask us to do away with "the picnic" completely. It does not ask us to live in a world without pleasure, fun, sex, and creativity. The Christian revolution places these things in their correct place within the created order.

CHRISTIANITY'S REVOLUTION UNDERSTANDS THAT THE RULER WHO MUST BE DEPOSED IN THIS CHRISTIAN REVOLUTION IS THE SELF—THE HUMAN

INDIVIDUAL WHO ULTIMATELY WISHES TO BE A GOD, WHO THROUGH THEIR STRIVING DISRUPTS THE CREATED ORDER AND TURNS CREATIVITY, SEXUALITY, AND PLEASURE INTO ENDS IN THEMSELVES.

Christianity brought into the world a strange and wonderful new freedom. Through Christ's death upon the cross, we not only won freedom from ourselves, we also received something—our true selves back. It was a staggering freedom, one that we bucked and fought against. At times Christians and the church would forget this freedom, slipping back into pagan modes of power and chaos. This freedom, however, opened a new world. It was the foundation upon which the West was built. Yet over time, the forces of counterrevolution would amass. The tyranny of self would again rear its head, eventually taking power of the cultural landscape of the West. Rod Dreher claims,

> We have ceased to believe in the Christian cultural framework, yet we have made it impossible to believe in any other that does

what culture must do: restrain individual passions and channel them creatively toward communal purposes . . . Our post-Christian culture, then, is an "anti-culture." We are compelled by the logic of modernity and the myth of individual freedom to continue tearing away the last vestiges of the old order, convinced that true happiness and harmony will be ours once all limits have been nullified.[5]

SMARTPHONES GET SMARTER, THE WORLD GETS MORE CHAOTIC

We find ourselves then in a strange place at the onset of the twenty-first century. Our public lives are now lived under the heroic myth. Power, control, and violence are still the tools of the state. Buildings keep getting built, our smartphones get smarter, technology continues its march toward the horizon, and we have the freedom to indulge our desires. Yet while our public life is ordered, our private lives reflect chaos. We again attempt to hold the *chaoskampf* in tension. We can be successful in our jobs, yet our private lives can be filled with addictions and anxiety. Our search for absolute freedom has left us entrapped. Our skyscrapers stand tall, but the winds of cultural chaos, whipped up by our own narcissistic desires to go it alone, lash at our souls. This is our cultural storm.

In such a time and such a place, the healing power of biblical leadership is desperately needed. In a world in which individual pleasure is everything, in which pain is avoided, the biblical leader with eyes upon the cross walks hand in hand with God into suffering and pain.

IN A CULTURE THAT IS INCREASINGLY FRAGMENTARY, EPISODIC, AND CONFUSED, THE BIBLICAL LEADER ACKNOWLEDGES A SWEEPING COSMIC DRAMA, A NARRATIVE THAT BINDS TOGETHER THE UNIVERSE.

In a time in which the individual's rights and desires are unquestioned, the biblical leader lives as a slave to Christ, looking to His guidance rather than personal preference in order to make decisions. In a society of the spectacle, which reduces everything and everyone to the superficial, the biblical leader cultivates an inner world, born out of a communion with the living God. The biblical leader's words, actions, attitudes, and behaviors are a witness to Jesus' victory on the cross and His resurrection on the third day.

STRONGER THAN HITLER

Three artists sit in the dark with a creative leader. The storm breaking above their heads was not a storm of falling water but of bombs.
Their silence was not one born of anticipation but of reverence.
They were stunned by what they had just heard. In a small apart-
ment in St. Petersburg, surrounded by sheet music and three friends,
a small, bookish man in his early thirties had just feverishly played a
piece of music. As his fingers fought with the keys, he seemed a ball
of stress and excitement. As the air raid sirens wailed, and as the German bombs dropped, the man kept playing. To his watching friend
it seemed as if the "music, the roar of the guns, the fires springing up,
the bombs, the sirens, the planes—all seemed to . . . blend into a cacophony in which reality and art were inextricably linked."[6] Dimitri
Shostakovich had just written his new symphony.

It is the Paris premiere for which *The Rite of Spring* is remembered, but it was St. Petersburg, known as the Paris of the East, in
which the work was created. Yet now it was no longer 1913; everything had changed.

Its choreographer, Nijinsky, no longer tantalized audiences with
his sexually suggestive performances. Just after the war he had attempted to dance the war for an audience, and not long after he
descended into a mental breakdown.

Isadora Duncan, the radical American dancer of the troupe,
who attempted to use dance to promote Nietzsche's philosophy,
had been killed in spectacular fashion. As she rode in her convert-
ible her fashionably long scarf, ostentatiously blowing in the wind
behind her, had caught in the tire and whipped her out of the car,
smashing her into the French boulevard.

The composer, Igor Stavinksy, had dreamed of a piece centered
on a pagan ceremony, which became the radically, modern, atonal
score of *The Rite of Spring*. Living in Paris, his wife and daughter

dead, no longer did radical breaks with tradition excite him. After reading the Gospels, the man who had unleashed, the man who had shocked Paris with his fusion of the pagan and the modern, had become a Christian. He now created symphonies based upon the Psalms.

It was this symphony of Psalms that had inspired Dimitri Shostakovich, the man playing the piano during the air raid. Shostakovich, living during the worst years of Soviet dictator Joseph Stalin's reign of terror, had found art of composing a life and death game. Millions would lose their lives under Stalin's rule. Solomon Volkov made the comment, "For many years, Shostakovich and his family balanced precariously on the edge of catastrophe, under constant threat of arrest, exile, or worse."[7] St. Petersburg, created as a capital of art and culture, had been renamed Leningrad by the Soviets. Stalin despised the city. Under his regime thousands of its citizens would disappear, taken by the secret police, never to be seen again. On September 8, 1941, Nazi troops surrounded the city, beginning history's worst siege of a city. Leningrad would be cut off from the world for almost nine hundred days. Hitler's plan to turn Eastern Europe into "living space" for his new society was seen in its starkest form as the plan was given to wipe the city of two and a half million people off the map. By the end of the siege, the population would sink to below a million. If the vitality of spring had been the motif of modernity at the beginning of the twentieth century, a winter of death would mark the war in Russia. Cut off from food, reinforcements, and supplies, the Nazis added the weapon of starvation to their morbid arsenal. People would drop dead mid-sentence; their relatives, so used to death, would keep eating. One of the most chilling mementoes of the war is the diary of Tanya, a twelve-year-old girl found alone in her home, surrounded by the corpses of her family. Its childish handwriting scrawls,

Zhenya died on Dec. 28th at 12:00 P.M. 1941
Grandma died on Jan. 25th 3:00 P.M. 1942
Leka died on March 5th at 5:00 A.M. 1942
Uncle Vasya died on Apr. 13th at 2:00 after midnight 1942
Uncle Lesha on May 10th at 4:00 P.M. 1942
Mother on May 13th at 7:30 A.M. 1942
Savichevs died.
Everyone died.
Only Tanya is left.[8]

Tanya herself would not survive the war. As the Germans attacked, the city still lived in fear of their own government's secret police. Generals who valiantly defended the city and secured food for their own citizens would be executed on Stalin's orders for not asking for help in the correct manner. The city was caught between Stalin, his soviet regime—built upon science, technology, a denial of the spiritual, and a cult of the hero leader embodied in Stalin— and Nazism, built upon Romantic idealism, spirituality, demonic destructiveness and led by the embodiment of Nietzche's vision of the artist-tyrant, Adolf Hitler. Leningrad was caught in the *chaoskampf*. In this storm of unparalleled chaos, Dimitri Shostakovich would emerge, proving that strange times create strange leaders.

Working as a fireman during the day, Shostakovich quickly composed his Symphony No. 7 named "Leningrad." "I couldn't not write it," he would say. It was not just a piece that was written against Hitler, but it was written about other enemies of humanity. The war had brought much pain and sorrow, but the piece was also about the destruction that had begun in the time before the war. It was an elegy, opposite in spirit to *The Rite of Spring*, not celebrating the destructive act but instead mourning destruction and loss of life. With the Soviet repression of religion and the churches closed, there was nowhere for the people to go to look for solace, to process their grief and pain. Shostakovich went against the anti-Semitic climate that was sweeping Europe and began to study Jewish folk music. He would write in his diary, "Jewish folk music has made a most powerful impression on me. I never tire of delighting in it, it's multi-faceted, it can appear to be happy while it is tragic. It's . . . laughter through tears."[9] Stranvinsky's symphony of the Psalms would lead Shostakovich to study the psalms of David, the king who in Psalm 18 was besieged by his enemies and encountered God in a storm. Shostakovich's biographer, Solomon Volkov notes, "He had to find the path from individual feelings to common ones, and to express his hidden emotions in a way that would make them accessible to the audience and allow it to experience catharsis . . . that it would be the 'cleansing storm.'"[10] Shostakovich would write in his dedication, "To the historic confrontation now taking place between reason and obscuratism, culture and barbarity, light and dark."[11]

On August the second, 1942, Shostakovich's symphony was performed in Leningrad. When the attack upon Leningrad had begun, Hitler had boasted that on that date, he would hold a party at the Leningrad Astoria, going as far as having invitations printed. During a preperformance, as the conductor, Karl Eliasberg, had raised his hand to begin, one oboist remembered, "When he raised his arms his hands shook. I had this feeling that he was a bird that had just been shot, that at any moment he would plummet to the ground."[12] During practices, musicians would regularly collapse from exhaustion and starvation. So terrible was the rate of death that a rule was made that even if one's spouse passed away in the night, one must turn up to practice. So terrible were the practices, it seemed that the performance would be an impossibility. Yet on the morning of the performance, the players seemed to wake with an unusual strength. A Russian bombardment of German positions began to allow the concert to proceed. The hall filled with a bedraggled mass of survivors. The remnants of Leningrad's orchestra slowly moved onto the stage, their clothes hanging off their skeletal frames. The performance began and the audience was spiritually transported away from the siege, lifted upon a transcendent wave of music. For ninety minutes, the reservoir of emotion held back by the twin Nazi and Soviet forces of tyranny burst forth in a flood of cathartic tears. "When the piece ended . . . there was not a sound in the hall—silence. Then someone clapped at the back, then another, then there was thunder."[13] One of the clarinet players, recounted that he can "still hear the thunder of applause from the audience. That will be the last image before my eyes when I die."[14]

Loudspeakers had been placed outside of the city, projecting the performance at the German troops. It is said that after hearing the concert, many of the German troops realized that they would not be able to defeat the city. *The Rite of Spring*, performed in Paris, a city of vibrancy and beauty, had proclaimed destruction and death. Shostakovich's Seventh Symphony, written and performed in a city of destruction and death, proclaimed resurrection and life. *The Rite of Spring* was art as life, the seventh symphony was art that brought life.

At the Moscow premiere of the piece, the writer Olga Berggolts, mourning the loss of her husband and suffering of her country, a weeping mess after sitting through Symphony No. 7, looked down from her seat. She saw Shostakovich with his glasses and his mop of hair, a man wedged between two monstrous tyrannies with nothing but his creativity and his Psalms, and thought, "This man is stronger than Hitler."[15]

THE REBUILDERS

Over the six weeks of my fast I began to change. The pounds dropped off me, but something was changing inside of me. I was in a storm and it was painful. However, I came to realize that in a storm, God shreds you of those parts of you that battle Him. Those who avoid God's holy storms fail to feel their pain, but they also fail to grow. They fail to meet the God in the storm, the One who asks His leaders to die to everything. By the end of the six weeks I was exhausted yet at peace.

As my friends and coworkers returned from their summer escapes, all mentioned that I had changed in a profound way. No longer were people looking to me because of my gifts and talents. My ministry was now directly flowing out of my personal battle through my surrendering to God in it. My life was now my sermon, my book, my leadership. After David encounters God in the storm in Psalm 18:16–19 he writes,

> He reached down from on high and took hold of me;
>   he drew me out of deep waters.
> He rescued me from my powerful enemy,
>   from my foes, who were too strong for me.
> They confronted me in the day of my disaster,
>   but the Lord was my support.
> He brought me out into a spacious place;
>   he rescued me because he delighted in me.

Everything in the culture encouraged me to just throw in the towel and rage at God. Yet each Sunday I would turn up, share what God was teaching me, and something began to happen—something that seemed counterintuitive to everything that I had come to believe. That spacious place that I finally found was flowing out of me.

For almost my entire ministry life, I had never really been a part of or worked at a mainstream church. I was always on the forefront of how church should be structured. I had created all kinds of novel church plants, reimagined what church services could look like. I had planted a church in a cafe in the belief that it was rigid church organization and a lack of creativity and imagination that was keeping people away. This was as unlike church as you could get. It was a church fully wrapped around the organic values. After building a relationship with the owner, we met in the upstairs room of the cafe. People would dribble in, we got rid of worship altogether, and I would lead a discussion-based biblical teaching over coffee. However, I began to notice that our cafe in the public sphere seemed to attract disillusioned Christians. There were some keen and committed people attending, but it was not hard to feel as though we had created a space for Christians who had stopped going to church, yet who were happy to turn up twenty minutes late to this cafe meeting every few weeks. A liquid church in a liquid culture simply washes away.

I began to realize that it was easier to reimagine church structure than it is to reimagine what it means to live a life fully devoted to God in modern culture. It was easier to tear down than to allow God to rebuild me. In Psalm 18:32–36 David writes,

> It is God who arms me with strength
>   and keeps my way secure.
> He makes my feet like the feet of a deer;
>   he causes me to stand on the heights.
> He trains my hands for battle;
>   my arms can bend a bow of bronze.
> You make your saving help my shield,
>   and your right hand sustains me;
>   your help has made me great.
> You provide a broad path for my feet,
>   so that my ankles do not give way.

God takes His servants through storms to teach them how to prepare for battle. The heights were the dangerous places, where the pagans worshiped. Yet after meeting him in a storm, God would teach David to walk on those places with the feet of a deer, nimble and secure. Through my storm, I came to understand that God was calling me to build a church for those who wish to serve Him in the dangerous high places of the repaganizing West. To do this, however, we need leaders, influencers, and creatives who have met Him in the storm.

My friend Thomas Willer, a pastor and sociologist from Denmark, believes that we are on the verge of a generation of reconstructors. He points to the comeback of the computer games like Sim City and Lego, noting that for the current generation of young adults, the dominant "ground story" of their youth was Harry Potter, which is the story of a young boy with no family who defeats the chaotic, destructive evil of Lord Voldemort, giving his own life so that the world may be saved. The end point of the Harry Potter story centers on restored family and the continuation of tradition. The final image of the Potter saga features a grown Harry and his friends, now married and happy, sending their own children on the train to Hogwarts for the first time.

Around the world, within the church and outside of it, there is a grouping of people that remain largely unnamed. They are unnamed, ignored by the chattering classes because they quietly are getting on with the job. They are founding not-for-profits, planting churches, creating new ministries, starting new businesses, advocating for causes. Our culture of deconstruction no longer makes sense to them. The culture of deconstruction that has come to dominate the church no longer helps them. It hinders them. They are the rebuilders, partners with God in the rebuilding of His creational order.

So I sit here writing almost one year to the day that I started my fast, in the same old house on my church property. The old heater is still providing warmth, but almost everything else is different in the room. The walls are a fresh white. The old carpet is gone, replaced by beautiful wooden floorboards. The room, like our church, has been transformed physically and spiritually by the rebuilders.

Instead of worrying about moving from the mechanical values to the organic values, we simply began a culture of living wholeheartedly for the God we find in the storm. Without my direction, my church asked to follow my fast a month later. A group began meeting each Monday as I had, praying and waiting upon Him. Our church culture shifted from deconstruction to devotion. We began to grow and flourish. No longer did we just attract disillusioned Christians, we began to attract the very kinds of people who I had attempted to reach all those years ago, when I first attended that postmodern conference. We began to fill with rebuilders.

I still have bipolarity. However, now that my twins are a little bit older, the routine nature of family life has helped my condition and kept my moods stable. And so as I type these final words, the heater warms my feet, and I can truly say with David,

> You exalted me above my foes;
>   from a violent man you rescued me.
> Therefore I will praise you, Lord, among the nations;
>   I will sing the praises of your name. (Psalm 18:48–49)

NOTES

PART I

1. Albert Speer, *Inside the Third Reich* (New York: Macmillan, 1970), 248–349.
2. Clay Shirky, *Here Comes Everybody* (New York: Penguin, 2009), 122–23.
3. David Brooks, *Bobos in Paradise: The New Upper Class and How They Got There* (New York: Simon & Schuster, 2000), 132.
4. Roman Guardini, *The End of the Modern World* (Wilmington, DE: ISI Books, 1956), 36.
5. Robin Lane Fox, *Pagans and Christians* (London: Penguin, 1986).
6. Peter Gay, *The Enlightenment: The Rise in Modern Paganism* (New York: Norton, 1966).

PART II

1. Jules Verne, *20,000 Leagues Under the Sea* (New York: Grosset & Dunlop, 1917), 1.
2. Ibid., 3.
3. Ibid., 3.
4. Ibid., 62.
5. Ibid., 69.
6. Ibid., 64.
7. Roland Barthes, *Mythologies* (London: Vintage, 2009), 74.
8. Ibid., 74.
9. Arthur Rimbaud, "The Drunken Boat," translated by Wallace Fowlie, The Poetry Foundation. www.poetryfoundation.org/poem/242790.

PART III

1. Walter Benjamin, *Arcades Project*, translated by Howard Eilan and Kevin McLaughlin (Cambridge, MA and London: Harvard University Press, 1999), 7.
2. Henry Adams, *The Education of Henry Adams* (Radford, VA: Wilder Publications, 2009), ebook.
3. Colin Jones, *Paris: Biography of a City* (London: Allen Lane, 2004), 407–8.

4. W. H. Auden quoted in Alan Bloom, *Shakespeare: Invention of the Human* (London: Fourth Estate, 1998), 419.

5. Guy de Maupassant, *A Parisian Affair and Other Stories* (London: Penguin, 2004), 41.

6. Ibid., 42.

7. Ibid., 42.

8. Ibid., 43.

9. Ibid., 46.

10. Ibid., 47.

11. Émile Zola, *The Kill* (New York: Random House, 2004), 8.

12. Ibid., 8–9.

13. Ibid., 11–12.

14. Charles Baudelaire, "The Flowers of Evil," Fleursdumal.org, http://fleursdumal.org/poem/099.

PART IV

1. Richard Mouw, *When the Kings Come Marching In: Isaiah and the New Jerusalem* (Grand Rapids, MI: Eerdmans, 2002), ebook.

2. Ibid.

3. Phillip Cary, *Jonah: Brazos Theological Commentary on the Bible* (Grand Rapids, MI: Brazos, 2008), 27.

4. Henry Richard Blackaby, *Spiritual Leadership: Moving People on to God's Agenda* (Nashville: B&H, 2011), 40.

5. Jacques Ellul, *The Judgment of Jonah* (Grand Rapids, MI: Eerdmans, 1971), 22.

6. Cary, *Jonah*, 47.

7. Ibid., 47.

8. Herman Melville, *Moby Dick* (New York: Random House, 1991), 62.

9. Ibid.

10. Ellul, *Judgment*, 35.

11. Ibid., 33.

PART V

1. Augusta Webb quoted in Tim Jeal, *Stanley: The Impossible Life of Africa's Greatest Explorer* (Yale University Press, 2008), 145.

2. Henry Morton Stanley, *How I Found Livingstone* (Mineola, NY: Courier Dover Publications, 2002), 330.

3. Ibid., 331.

4. Ibid.

5. Tim Jeal, *Stanley*, 155.

6. George Washington Williams quoted in Adam Hochschild, *King Leopold's Ghost* (Boston: Houghton Mifflin Harcourt, 1999), ebook.

7. Philipp Blom, *The Vertigo Years: Change and Culture in the West, 1900–1914* (Toronto: McCelland & Stewart, 2008), 187.

8. Abraham Kuyper, *Lectures on Calvinism* (Peabody, MA: Hendrickson, 2008), 17.

9. Ibid.

10. Thomas à Kempis, *The Imitation of Christ* (London: Penguin Classics, 1952), 39.

11. Enuma Elish, The Epic of Creation, trans. L. W. King, from The Seven Tablets of Creation, London, 1902. http://www.sacred-texts.com/ane/enuma. htm.

12. Timothy K. Beal, *Religion and Its Monsters* (New York: Routledge, 2002), 18.

13. Jonathan and Christopher Nolan, *The Dark Knight* (Burbank, CA: Warner Bros. Pictures, 2008).

14. Victor Hugo, *Les Miserables* (London: Vintage, 2009), 1181.

15. Hochschild, *Ghost*.

16. Joseph Conrad, *Heart of Darkness* (London: Penguin, 1995), 95.

17. Hochschild, *Ghost*.

18. William Shakespeare, *The Twelfth Night* (New Delhi: Atlantic Publishers, 2007), 138.

19. Daniel Boostin, *The Image: A Guide to Pseudo-Events in America* (New York: Vintage, 1961), 45.

20. Ibid., 45.

21. T. S. Eliot, "The Hollow Men," All Poetry. http://allpoetry.com/poem/8453753-The_Hollow_Men-by-T_S__Eliot.

22. A. N. Wilson, *The Victorians* (London: Arrow, 2002), 488.

PART VI

1. This story is found in Rod Thompson and Athalia Bond, "The World is Your Playground: Competing Stories of Gospel and Globalized Adventure" in Michael W. Goheen and Erin G. Glanville, eds., *The Gospel and Globalization* (Vancouver, BC, Regent College Publishing, 2009).

2. Paul Zweig quoted in Christopher Lasch, *The Culture of Narcissism: American Life in an Age of Diminishing Expectations* (New York: Warner, 1980), 24–25.

3. Arnold J. Toynbee, *A Study of History* (London: Oxford University Press, 1946).

4. Adam Curtis discussed this concept in his presentation at the Story Conference in February, 2011.

5. Henri J. M. Nouwen, *In the Name of Jesus: Reflections on Christian Leadership* (New York: Crossroad, 1989), 54.

6. Edwin H. Friedman, *A Failure of Nerve: Leadership in the Age of the Quick Fix* (New York: Church Publishing, 2007).

PART VII

1. Charles Baudelaire, *The Painter of Modern Life and Other Essays (Arts and Letters)* (London: Phaidon, 1995), 5.
2. Ibid., 29.
3. Periodical quoted in Tim Blanning, *The Romantic Revolution* (London: Phoenix, 2010), 39.
4. Jerrold Seigel, *Bohemian Paris: Culture, Politics, and the Boundaries of Bourgeois Life, 1830–1930* (Baltimore: Johns Hopkins University Press, 1986), 240.
5. Ibid.
6. Albert Camus, *The Rebel* (London:Penguin, 1971), 51.
7. Heath and Potter quoted in Sieigel, *Bohemian*, 239.
8. Albert Camus, *The Rebel* (London: Penguin, 1971), 47.
9. See Jean Jacques Rousseau, *A Discourse on the Moral Effects of the Arts and Sciences*, Bartleby.com. www.bartleby.com/168/503.html.
10. Blanning, *Revolution*, 26.
11. Lewis Mumford, *The Condition of Man* (New York: Harvest, 1944), 299–300.
12. Ibid., 300.
13. Camus, *Rebel*, 50.
14. John Milton, *Paradise Lost* (Oxford: Oxford University Press, 2004), 11.
15. Richard John Neuhaus, *The Naked Public Square: Religion and Democracy in America* (Grand Rapids, MI: Eerdmans, 1984), 82.
16. John Micklethwait and Adrian Wooldridge, *God Is Back: How the Global Revival of Faith Is Changing the World* (New York: Penguin, 2009), 33.

PART VIII

1. Judith Mackrell, "The Rite of Spring at Sadler's Wells," *The Guardian*, April 4, 2013. www.guardian.co.uk/stage/2013/apr/03/rite-of-spring-sadlers-wells.
2. Modris Eksteins, *Rites of Spring: The Great War and the Birth of the Modern Age* (New York: Mariner, 1989), 14.
3. Dorothy L. Sayers quoted in *Dante, The Divine Comedy 2: Purgatory* (London: Penguin, 1955), 43.
4. Aaron Betsky quoted in Jane Pavitt, *Brand.New* (London, V & A, 2000), 116.
5. Eksteins, *Rites*, 60.
6. Beaudelaire, *Painter*, 9.
7. Mary Eberstadt, *How the West Really Lost God* (West Conshohocken, PA: Templeton Press, 2013).
8. Bruno Hahnel quoted in Laurence Rees, *The Dark Charisma of Adolf Hitler: Leading Millions into the Abyss* (London: Ebury Publishing, 2013), 43.
9. Jon Savage, *Teenage: The Prehistory of Youth Culture 1875–1945* (London: Penguin, 2007), 47.

10. Eksteins, *Rites*, 87.
11. Heinrich Heine quoted in Eric Metaxes, *Bonhoeffer: Pastor, Martyr, Prophet, Spy* (Nashville: Thomas Nelson, 2010), 103–4.
12. Paul Fussell, *The Great War and Modern Memory* (New York: Oxford University Press, 2000), 8.
13. Ian Kershaw, *Hitler* (London: Penguin, 1998), 936.
14. Putzi Hanfstaengl quoted in Kershaw, *Hitler*, 210.
15. Albert Speer, *Third Reich*, 297.
16. Ibid., 403–4.
17. Camus, *Rebel*, 46.
18. Kershaw, *Hitler*, xxxvi.
19. Eksteins, *Rites*, 319.
20. Joseph Goebbels quoted in Eksteins, *Rites*, 328.
21. Eksteins, *Rites*, 328.

PART IX

1. Abraham J. Heschel, *The Prophets* (New York, HarperPerennial, 2001), 7.
2. Mumford, *Condition*, 294.
3. Hugo, *Les Miserables*, 592.
4. David Bentley Hart, *Atheist Delusions: The Christian Revolution and Its Fashionable Enemies* (New Haven, CT: Yale University Press, 2009), 108.
5. Rod Dreher, "Sex After Christianity," *The American Conservative*, April 11, 2013. www.theamericanconservative.com/articles/sex-after-christianity/.
6. Harrison E. Salisbury, *The 900 Days: The Siege of Leningrad* (New York: Harper & Row, 1969), 298.
7. Solomon Volkov, *Shostakovich and Stalin* (New York: Knopf, 2004), vii.
8. History in an Hour, "Only Tanya is left—the short life of Tanya Savicheva," January 25, 2010. www.historyinanhour.com/2010/01/25/tanya-savicheva-summary/.
9. Solomon Volkov, ed., *Testimony: The Memoirs of Dmitri Shostakovich* (New York: Limelight Editions, 1979), 156.
10. Volkov, Shostakovich and Stalin, 208–9.
11. Shostakovich quoted in Ed Vulliamy, "Orchestra Manoeuvres," The Guardian, November 24, 2001. www.guardian.co.uk/theobserver/2001/nov/25/features.magazine27.
12. Anna Reid, *Leningrad: The Epic Siege of World War II, 1941–44* (London, Bloomsbury, 2011), 361.
13. Mrs. Matus quoted in Vulliamy, "Orchestra."
14. Viktor Koslov quoted in Vulliamy, "Orchestra."
15. Olga Berggolts quoted in Salisbury, *900 Days*, 522.

ACKNOWLEDGMENTS

A book is written by an author but in reality is a team effort. So much thanks to the following people:

The fantastic Moody team in Chicago—Randall Payleitner, Natalie Mills, Jesse Lipes, Bailey Utecht, Brittany Biggs, and Pam Pugh. My wife, Trudi Sayers, for love and doing the hard yards behind the scenes. Matt Deutscher, for a great cover. Sarah Deutscher, for reading the manuscript and providing invaluable feedback. Jon Tyson, for the foreword and being my stateside champion. Bethany Dickins, for hunting down books at libraries for me. The wonderful people at Red Church, for support and encouragement. Terry Walling, for being a lighthouse in the storm.

Enjoy this complimentary excerpt of
The Road Trip That Changed the World,
another book by Mark Sayers.

* * *

ONE:

A TALE OF TWO ROADS

"Whither goest thou, America, in thy shiny car in the night?"
Carlo Marx in Jack Kerouac's On the Road

"Nobody move, everything will be OK."
Mohamed Atta

In their chinos, casual shirts, and T-shirts they even dressed like writer Jack Kerouac. And although they had probably never read his classic novel *On the Road,* they were imitating Kerouac's vision of life to a T, living in cheap motels, sleeping in rental cars, criss-crossing their way around America. Through their lifelong exposure to popular culture, they had imbibed the life script for twentysome-things that Kerouac had sketched out almost half a century earlier. They were in a limbo, existing on the American road.

A delayed adolescence marked the culture of their group. Theirs was an all-male world. Yet long-distance phone calls to girlfriends, parents, and neglected wives betrayed an internal conflict between a desire for domestic bliss and an unfettered pursuit of pleasure. Kerouac was drawn to the seedy side of American life, so were the boys, they also liked strip clubs and dive bars. In Florida they rented scooters, speeding up and down the beaches.

They also seemed to have a weakness for glazed donuts, visiting convenience stores to sugar-load several times a day.[1]

The group had traveled en masse to Las Vegas, where they stayed in "cheap hotels on a dreary stretch of the Strip frequented by dope dealers and $10 street hookers."[2] The sons of the wealthy were slumming it, and just like Kerouac would regularly be seen staggering drunk or stoned on hash. Other nights they would go up-market and splash the cash on lap dances and expensive champagnes.[3]

Their public displays of arrogance and excess ensured that women would be seen on their arms. When they were not in the clubs they were buying porn,[4] and paying for sex with prostitutes in their hotel rooms. Their behavior could have been the script for an MTV reality show or a B-grade spring break movie, a lifestyle unintentionally championed by Kerouac on the fringes of American life. A vision of life that would in our time be pushed to the center, becoming typical and expected.

Yet these men were far from typical. Their wild living was a precursor of something more sinister.

A COCKTAIL OF FAITH AND VICE

Jack Kerouac lived out a contradiction. Raised a conservative Catholic, he maintained a love for and relationship with Christ for his whole life. Even in his most debauched moments his Bible was never far from his side. At times he was prudish and conservative, at other times a libertine. The young men in the group were the same. Like Kerouac, their actions were also contradictory. One moment they were deeply religious, praying late into the night and poring over scriptures; the next moment their behavior was marked by an unrestrained indulgence in vice.

Both Kerouac and the young men were drawn to and yet felt like outsiders in American life. Both wished for a death that would see them leave this world and find union with God in paradise.

Kerouac's journey to find God would take the form of a modern pilgrimage, with off-ramps and excursions into drug-fueled hallucinations, and dalliances with Buddhism and Taoism. Eventually, his body broken and addicted, he would return to his childhood devotion, spending his last days focused on Christ and the Cross. The young men would take a very different road in their quest to please God.

GO, GO, GO!

Popular culture chooses to ignore the middle-aged, worn-out Kerouac, hip to the futility of the American dream and the reality of sin, spending his last days meditating on the Cross. Instead it prefers the romantic vision of the handsome, twentysomething seminal hipster of *On the Road*. Speeding across America in a beat-up car that flew like a rocket, high as a kite, pretty girls in the back, jazz pouring out of the radio. His wild buddy and partner in crime Neal Cassady next to him like a fan at a jazz club, screaming GO, GO, GO out the window into the impossibly starry expanse of the Midwestern sky.

> THAT MORNING THE NEW YORK STREETS THAT KEROUAC HAD WALKED HALF A CENTURY EARLIER WITH HIS FRIENDS WERE SHOWERED IN THE CONCRETE DUST OF THE WORLD TRADE CENTER.

The young men would also be remembered for posterity, flying across America at high speed, not on an impossibly starry night, but on an impossibly blue-skied morning. Their shouts would not be jazz-inspired slang. Instead they would be guttural and Arabic, screamed last words of *"Allahu Akbar."* That morning the New York streets that Kerouac had walked half a century earlier with his friends were showered in the concrete dust of the World Trade Center and the vaporized remains of Mohamed Atta and his friends, known to history as the 9/11 hijackers.

CONTRADICTIONS

To us the behavior of the 9/11 hijackers seems strange. These were terrorists. A group of militants committed to a radical interpretation of Islam. A cell of men who were ready to offer their lives to defeat an enemy that they saw as morally degenerate. Men whose idea of modesty ensured that they covered with towels frames on their walls that contained some old photos of women bathing in 1920s swimming costumes, yet who happily would visit strip clubs.

The contradictory behavior of the 9/11 hijackers has confused analysts. Yet when examined in the light of our culture's true nature, the behavior of the group is not that shocking. Humans are contradictory creatures: we like to be logical, but our actions, wants, and desires are a far more confusing and inconsistent affair.

The majority of the 9/11 attackers were from upper- or middle-class families. Many, like the group's leader Mohamed Atta, had spent time living and studying in the West and felt strongly the tension between the worldview of the West and their adherence and loyalty to their own worldview and religion. The propaganda of Al Qaeda would point to various rationales for its war on the West, such as Western foreign policy, the existence of the state of Israel, and so on, but the hijackers' last moments giving into temptation illustrates a deeper and more implicit motive. They viewed the West as a culture that had thrown off any kind of restraint. Their last gasp giving into the fleshly temptations of the West was an admission to its seductive power and a confirmation of its need to be destroyed. Christianity and Judaism were seen as impotent and inferior because they had failed to rein in this new secular self with all of its base desires and personal freedoms.

The hijackers unintentionally found themselves caught between

two visions of being human that would come to dominate the consciousness of the world at the beginning of the twenty-first century.
To understand this tension more fully and appreciate its pull, not
just on the lives of the 9/11 hijackers but on our own, we must now
travel back to the period just after World War II. Back to the same
Manhattan streets that Mohamed Atta would cover in ash, streets
that in 1948 two men walked, reveling in and wrestling with the new
culture that was emerging in the West. Two men who would create
two philosophical roads.

TAKING A TEMPTING BITE OUT OF THE BIG APPLE

During a two-year period between 1947 and 1948, two young men
lived in New York City. Both men were aspiring writers, both had
reached a crossroads in their personal lives, both felt that Western
culture had descended into a spiritual and existential crisis. Both
men would end up writing bestselling books about this experience,
works that would electrify generations to come, mold lifestyles, and
offer visions of being human that would help shape the twenty-first
century. Both in their own way would leave their marks not only on
New York but on global culture. Both men would die early, in a manner that would appear as a kind of martyrdom to their followers.
Their ideas would live on long after their deaths.

WHO WAS JACK KEROUAC?

Journalist Tom Brokaw would label Jack Kerouac's peers the
"greatest generation," lauding their selflessness, work ethic, and
commitment. This was the generation who understood material
deprivation during the Great Depression, confronted the forces of
fascism during World War II, and during the forties and fifties built
America into the dominant global superpower.

　　Born in 1922, Kerouac was part of Brokaw's greatest generation, but his influence would shape the generation following his own. In a period of conformity and conservatism Kerouac would bounce around New York City in a ball of drug-fueled, jazz-inspired, sexual energy. Though unusual and deviant at the time, his lifestyle was far more like the typical young adults' of the twenty-first century—a lifestyle defined by a thirst for experience and travel, recreational drug use, a fear of and yet a desire for community and commitment. A promiscuous approach to sexuality, a desire to make it, a contradictory approach to faith, and few qualms about returning home to Mom when the money ran out.

For Kerouac, New York City was simply a starting point on a manic journey that would last for four years and that would criss-cross the United States multiple times. This journey, part spiritual quest, part hedonistic romp, would inspire every road movie. Every buddy flick, every spring break bender, and every twentysomething, backpacking search to discover one's self that would follow over the coming decades owes something to Kerouac and his vision. Without Kerouac there could be no *Easy Rider*, no *Eat, Pray, Love*, no *Blue Like Jazz*. The details of this odyssey would be transformed into Kerouac's famous book *On the Road*, which is part confessional, part travelogue, and part novel.

> **WITHOUT KEROUAC THERE COULD BE NO *EASY RIDER*, NO *EAT, PRAY, LOVE*, NO *BLUE LIKE JAZZ*.**

The book would be loosely autobiographical. *On the Road* tells the story of Kerouac and his friend Neal Cassady's numerous romps across the continental United States between 1947 and 1951. Since the book includes frank descriptions of the drug-fueled sexual misadventures of Kerouac's friends, his publishers worried about possible lawsuits. So they persuaded him to change the names to pseudonyms. Kerouac reinvented himself as Sal Paradise, and Neal became the legendary Dean Moriarty.

CATHOLIC, FRENCH-CANADIAN, AND CALVINIST

Kerouac was christened Jean Louis Lebris de Kerouac to French
Canadian parents in Lowell, Massachusetts. Growing up in a
French-speaking household, he did not speak English until he
was six. The defining moment of his life was the tragic death of
his brother Gerard from rheumatic fever at age nine. A survivor's
sense of guilt haunted Kerouac for the rest of his life. His mother
and father both loved God and the bottle—influences that would
mark Kerouac's life and shape his grief. The
French-speaking Catholics of Massachusetts
followed the teachings of Cornelius Jansen,
whose Catholicism was deeply influenced by
the theology of John Calvin. This unique blend
of Catholicism and Calvinism shaped Kerouac's

> IF AMERICA WAS
> SETTLING DOWN
> BEHIND WHITE PICKET
> FENCES, THEY WANTED
> A LIFE ON THE ROAD.

faith, infusing it with a deep understanding of sin, the Cross, and
the place of suffering in the Christian life.

A gifted football player, Kerouac earned a scholarship to Columbia University in Manhattan. Despite his athletic prowess and
good looks, Kerouac found a home amongst a strange grouping
of bohemian University buddies. The embryonic group consisted
of poet Allen Ginsberg, writer William S. Burroughs, editor Lucien
Carr, and various other misfits, bohemians, and artists. The group
was united in their belief that American culture had gone awry.
Their reading of Oswald Spengler's *Decline of the West* convinced
them that they were living at the end of Western culture.

The group looked at a postwar society awash in material-
ism, secularism, and shallowness, and came to the belief that if
rationalism and science had led society to its current crisis, then
romanticism, spirituality, and experience would re-humanize
America. The group found what they perceived as the strict and
conservative moral confines of the forties stifling. They began to

plot, plan, and live out a new way of being human, a response to the great crisis they saw all around them. If America was settling down behind white picket fences, they wanted a life on the road.

HOW A GROUP OF JAZZ FANS
SHAPED THE CONTEMPORARY SELF

The proximity of Columbia University to Harlem gave the group an appreciation of jazz and a somewhat naive and patronizing desire to imitate what they saw as the unfettered and authentic lives of African-Americans. This group of renegade bookworms also idolized other groups that they saw living on the edge of American culture, such as prostitutes, homosexuals, and petty criminals. Idolization would turn into imitation and eventually immersion as the group pushed the boundaries of acceptable social behavior, grounding themselves in the world of hustlers who hung around Times Square.

Unbeknownst to the group, their seminal experiments with sexuality, Eastern religions, drugs, and restless travel would be launched from the margins into the cultural mainstream over the coming decades. Kerouac labeled his friends the "Beat Genera-tion"; later the media would dub them "beatniks," after the Sput-nik satellite. The Beats would foreshadow the counterculture and the hippie movement of the sixties, which would in turn influence the mainstream in the seventies, and eventually come to define the contemporary consumer, popular culture, and personal quest-ing in the West.

TWO:

HOW WORSHIP BECAME ENTERTAINMENT

Not disciples but spectators . . .

During the same eighteen-month period in which Kerouac and his friends were instigating their new mode of living on the edge of American culture, a young, well-dressed man arrived in the Big Apple. Like Kerouac, he was an unsuccessful novelist; he had a group of friends who read voraciously and hung out in cafes. Like Kerouac he sensed a spiritual danger in the postwar economic boom. He also was in the midst of a personal crisis. Unlike Kerouac's existential crisis over the death of his brother, this young man's crisis was ideological in nature. Like Kerouac he had grown up in a religious home. Sayyid Qutb, however, had been moving toward a more radical understanding of Islam in his homeland of Egypt. Yet at the same time he was drawn to modernization, and the West. His residency in the United States would spiritually, ideologically, and emotionally push him to his limits.

AL QAEDA AND THE ALL-AMERICAN GIRL

While Kerouac would throw himself guiltily into the hedonism of emerging postwar America, Qutb would recoil from it. Qutb tells

235

the story of being woken on his ship over to America by a drunk woman who offered him sex. The encounter deeply shocked Qutb and shaped his interaction with and analysis of the United States. To Kerouac America was a seductress, inviting with her open expanses; spilling out westward she offered a new future of countless possibilities. To Qutb, America was a temptress sent by the devil to ensnare, entrap, and enslave. She was a danger, not just for the young, isolated, and homesick Muslim man but the entire Islamic world.

Sayyid, like Kerouac, could not help but notice the pulsating sexual energy of postwar America. The war had begun to change the social and sexual landscape. The conflict had taken young men away from women and a rediscovery of each other was occurring. Historian Robert S. Ellwood notes that the returning veterans brought back with them from the battlefields "newly uninhibited views on smoking, drinking, and sex."[1] The mobilization of women into the workforce during the war had given women a taste of equality, creating a new sense of boldness. This boldness was seductive to Kerouac who reveled in it with abandon. Qutb also noted this new spirit amongst mid-century American young women; however, to him it was repulsive, a sign of moral decay. In an essay on his time in America, Qutb wrote:

> The American girl is well acquainted with her body's seductive capacity. She knows it lies in the face, and in expressive eyes, and thirsty lips . . . she shows all this and does not hide it.[2]

The new American girl spoken of by Qutb could be readily found in the jazz clubs that Kerouac was drawn to. For Kerouac, jazz, particularly the sub-genre known as Bop, was transcendent, a kind of post-rational spiritual experience; an art form symbolic of a new future, and a new mode of humanity. Again Kerouac's view was in sharp contrast to Qutb, who offered this evaluation of American jazz music:

> The American is primitive. . . . Jazz music is his music of choice. It is this music that the savage bushmen created to satisfy their primitive desires, and their desire for noise on the one hand, and the abundance of animal noises on the other. The American's enjoyment of jazz does not fully begin until he couples it with singing like crude screaming. And the louder the noise of the voices and instruments, until it rings in the ears to an unbearable degree, the greater the appreciation of the listeners.[3]

Evaluating the responses of the two men, it would be easy at this point for us to write off Kerouac as a pioneer of the hedonism that has come to define youth and young adult culture in the West. It would also be equally tempting to dismiss Qutb's analysis as at best prudish and at worst bigoted. Both men, however, despite their limitations, noted cracks in Western culture that would turn into full-blown chasms. Both men through their writings would suggest new responses, new ways of being human that would radically change the spiritual landscape of the West.

KEROUAC'S ANSWER: THE RUCKSACK REVOLUTION

Kerouac would call for a "rucksack revolution," a generational move away from home on to the road, a new kind of lifestyle for young people that would be built upon experience, pleasure, spiritual exploration, mobility, and self-discovery. Kerouac would write that he saw "a vision of a great rucksack revolution thousands or even millions of young Americans wandering around with rucksacks."[4] For Kerouac this revolution would be a way of resisting what he saw as the secularizing and stupefying effects of mass consumer culture. His hope was founded in a sense that a new generation with a new vision for humanity, was:

> refusing to subscribe to the general demand that they consume production and therefore have to work for the privilege of consuming, all that . . . they didn't really want anyway such as refrigerators, TV sets, cars, at least new fancy cars, certain hair oils and deodorants and general junk you finally always see a week later in the garbage anyway, all of them imprisoned in a system of work, produce, consume, work, produce, consume.[5]

More than any other of his works, it was the publication of *On the Road* that would cast Kerouac into the media spotlight. The book would operate as a template for the new young-adult culture that would emerge over the coming decades. Slowly and surely his influence would be felt across New York, as his soft bohemianism would become the new mode of living communicated out from the city across the world through the channels of media, fashion, entertainment, and the industry of cool. Kerouac's unintended New York legacy can be found not just in the bars and cafes of Greenwich Village which he haunted, but also in the offices of MTV, *Playboy,* and Levis. In contrast Qutb would mostly be forgotten in New York. That is, until several decades later, when the young men of Al Qaeda, inspired by his writings, would fly commercial jets into both the World Trade Center towers and the consciousness of the West.

"ALL OF THEM IMPRISONED IN A SYSTEM OF WORK, PRODUCE, CONSUME, WORK, PRODUCE, CONSUME."

THE ROAD TO JIHAD

Qutb would also write a book based on his conclusions from his time in America, titled *Milestones*. Ironically Qutb would include a section in his work entitled "This Is the Road." Qutb's road was not Kerouac's open road of exploration; rather it was the road toward Shari'a law. Qutb not only would emerge from his time in America with a more radicalized view of Islam, he would become through his writings the spiritual guide of Al Qaeda's brand of Islam, personally inspiring the movement's two founders Ayman al-Zawahiri and Osama bin Laden. Virtually unknown in the West, Qutb would go on to be what the *Guardian* newspaper would label as "the most famous personality of the Muslim world in the second half of the 20th century."[6]

Living in the days after World War II, Qutb and Kerouac both sensed that a dramatic shift had occurred in Western culture. Both developed their own responses. Our journey in this book will follow Kerouac along his road—he will act as our guide to the culture that he helped create. Yet before we leave him behind, Qutb has some observations that will be foundational in our explorations of the way that our culture has shaped our lives and expressions of faith.

* * *

To read more of this book, get your copy of
The Road Trip That Changed the World, by Mark Sayers,
available at local and online retailers and on
www.ShopMoodyPublishers.com